Günter D. Roth

Weather Lore for Sailors and Windsurfers

EP Publishing Limited

8 — 11 — 95

About the author

Günter D. Roth was born in Munich in 1931. He had his first sailing experiences on the lakes of Upper Bavaria. As a student his main subject was economics, but he also had a special interest in astronomy and meteorology.

This interest was stimulated through lectures and his own observations.

The study of the sky and the weather has thus become his life-long hobby. His first book *Stars and Planets* was published in 1972, and was followed by *Weather Lore for Everyone* in 1976. Günter D. Roth is also editor of the *Star Enthusiast's Handbook* (3rd edition 1981) and joint editor of the monthly journal *Stars and the Universe*.

Published by EP Publishing Limited, Bradford Road, East Ardsley, Wakefield, WF3 2JN, England.

Translated by Andrew Shackleton
Illustrated by Barbara von Damnitz
Typeset in 10/11pt Times by
The Word Factory, Rossendale, Lancashire.
Printed and bound in Great Britain by Purnell and Sons (Book Production) Limited, Paulton, Bristol.

Originally published in German under the title *Praktische Wetterkunde für Segler, Surfer und Motorbootfahrer.*
Copyright © 1981 BLV Verlagsgesellschaft mbH, Munich.

English translation copyright © 1983 EP Publishing Limited.
First English edition 1983.
ISBN 0 7158 0869 9 (casebound)
ISBN 0 7158 0861 3 (paperback)

British Library Cataloguing in Publication Data

Roth, Günter D.
  Weather lore for sailors and windsurfers.
  1. Meteorology, Maritime 2. Yachts and yachting
  I. Title II. Praktische Wetterkunde für Segler, Surfer und Motorbootfahrer. *English*
  551.5′0246238   QC994
  ISBN 0-7158-0869-9
  ISBN 0-7158-0861-3 Pbk

Contents

Preface

Wind brings sailing to life. Sailing and windsurfing can only be enjoyable when there is enough wind. It is a form of energy, and though the wind is free you often have to wait for it. Sometimes, though, the wind blows so hard that boats have difficulty in coping with it. Storms can be fatal. In the Admiral's Cup disaster of 1979, 32 people died and more than 50 were injured. Such events are mercifully rare. But every year there are accidents from storms on the most apparently harmless of lakes. In most cases the sailor has simply failed to pay attention to the weather. Waves and breakers produced by the storms have often proved lethal to motor boats, too.

Every type of weather can be predicted. Wherever you are, whether on a lake or out at sea, there are countless opportunities for noting any changes in the weather. This may be from personal observations or from listening to weather reports on the radio.

This book gives a whole range of advice on the correct observation of wind, clouds and weather. It will also help you to understand the meteorological jargon used in weather reports and weather forecasts. When you have finished, try the questions in the appendix, to see how much you have learned. One preliminary observation: in this book I refer mostly to sailing, but what I say applies equally to the whole range of water sports. The observation and interpretation of the weather is of vital importance to sailors and windsurfers alike.

Günter D. Roth

What is weather?

Seafarers have always worried about the weather. This is particularly true of sailors, who depend for their propulsion on one important component of the weather, namely the wind. Sailing can also be affected by waves, swell and surf, which are produced by the weather. So too is fog, which causes particular problems for coastal sailing.

Weather lore is one part of the science of meteorology. All our weather happens within the earth's atmosphere, whether it is wind, cloud, thunder, rain or snow. It is to the atmosphere that we owe the blueness of the sky, the redness of sunsets and — indirectly — the many colours of the rainbow. The atmosphere is kept round the earth by the force of gravity. The changes and activities within the atmosphere are what we call weather. Four main elements are involved in this:

- Atmospheric pressure
- Temperature
- Wind
- Humidity

None of these factors is responsible on its own. The weather is determined by the combined action of all of them, with the result that it cannot be easily analysed. Most of the weather processes take place in the lower layers of the atmosphere, the area known as the troposphere. Troposphere means 'area of turbulence', which is an apt description of what goes on there. The troposphere is in continual movement. It also contains almost all of the water vapour to be found in the atmosphere. Water vapour and air currents are what produce clouds and rain.

The energy source for our weather is the sun. The heat of the sun reaches the earth's surface through the atmosphere. Some of this is radiated back into the atmosphere. The earth's surface acts like an enormous hotplate on the lower atmosphere, up to a height of about 1,500 metres. However, this transference of energy is extremely uneven. Quite apart from the varying position of the sun, we must consider the variable pattern of land and sea across the globe. Land and water behave quite differently in the way they absorb and reflect heat. Add to that the effect of mountain ranges, which interrupt and deflect the air-flow patterns. Friction with the ground is yet another influence on the lower atmosphere. The temperature falls on average in the troposphere by about $6-7C°$ for every 1,000 m above sea level. But this is very uneven for the first 1,500 m. Often the very opposite is

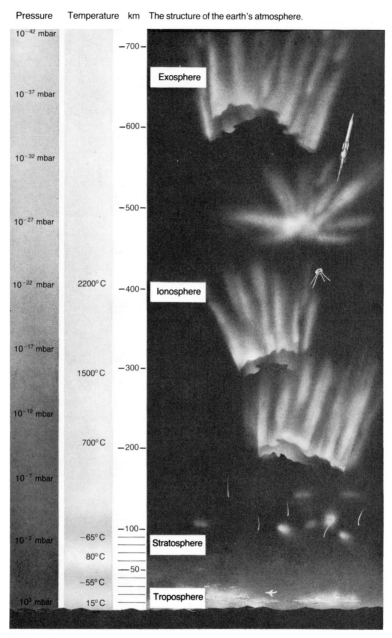

Pressure	Temperature	km	The structure of the earth's atmosphere.
10^{-42} mbar		$-700-$	Exosphere
10^{-37} mbar			
10^{-32} mbar		$-600-$	
10^{-27} mbar		$-500-$	
10^{-22} mbar	$2200°$ C	$-400-$	Ionosphere
10^{-17} mbar	$1500°$ C	$-300-$	
10^{-12} mbar	$700°$ C	$-200-$	
10^{-7} mbar			
10^{-2} mbar	$-65°$ C	$-100-$	Stratosphere
	$80°$ C		
	$-55°$ C	$-50-$	
10^{3} mbar	$15°$ C		Troposphere

Atmospheric pressure and temperature in the layers of the atmosphere.

true, with so-called **inversions** in which warm and cold air change places. The appearance of fog and haze boundaries is connected with this.

In comparison with the troposphere the higher layers of the atmosphere have a less immediate influence on our weather. That is to say, the stratosphere, which extends to about 50 km above sea level, plays a vital indirect role. For example, it absorbs most of the sun's ultraviolet rays and thus conveys heat to the troposphere.

Excluding water vapour, the atmosphere contains 78% nitrogen and 20% oxygen. The rest consists of various gases such as argon, ozone, hydrogen, carbon dioxide, helium and neon. Water vapour is not very abundant, and is variably distributed (3% over the tropical seas, but only 0.1% over the polar ice-caps). However, the transformation of water vapour into liquid rain and vice versa is bound up with the energy changes which produce weather.

Also to be found in the atmosphere are the whole range of what are called **condensation nuclei**. These are the tiny particles of dust, dirt and crystals which assist in the production of cloud and rain. The sailor will only become aware of these when the visibility becomes poor, or the sky becomes overcast.

Atmospheric pressure

The **barometer** is an essential piece of equipment for any boat. If the atmospheric pressure is rising or falling this will give us important information about the weather to come. It will, for example, tell us what the wind is going to do.

Atmospheric pressure is defined as the weight of the atmosphere upon a unit area at a particular point on the earth's surface. This involves the whole air column above this point, up as far as the furthest extreme of the atmosphere. The atmosphere exerts a pressure of about 1 kilogram weight on each square centimetre of the earth's surface. This fact was proved over 300 years ago by a pupil of Galileo called Torricelli.

Torricelli made his measurements by using a column of mercury held in equilibrium against the atmospheric pressure. Thus for a long time it became customary to measure atmospheric pressure in millimetres of mercury (abbreviated to mm Hg) or torrs. 1 mm Hg is the pressure exerted by a 1-mm-high column of mercury at freezing point.

At sea level the average atmospheric pressure is 760 mm Hg.

For many years now, the official units for the measurement of atmospheric pressure have been the bar and the millibar (usually abbreviated to mbar). 1 bar corresponds to 1,000 mbar. It also corresponds to 100,000 pascals (abbreviated to Pa), the SI unit of pressure.

The relationship between millibars and millimetres of mercury can be expressed thus:

1 mbar = 0.75 mm Hg or 1 mm Hg = 1.33 mbar.

The average atmospheric pressure at sea level is 1,013 mbar. The following conversion table may be of assistance:

Millimetres of mercury	Millibars	Inches of mercury
720	960	28.35
724	965	28.5
727.5	970	28.65
731	975	28.8
735	980	28.9
739	985	29.1
742.5	990	29.25
746	995	29.4
750	1,000	29.5
754	1,005	29.7
757.5	1,010	29.8
761	1,015	30.0
765	1,020	30.1
769	1,025	30.3
772.5	1,030	30.4
776	1,035	30.55
780	1,040	30.7

Atmospheric pressure decreases with height. In the lower atmosphere the decrease amounts to 1 mbar for every 8 m. At 6,000 m the atmospheric pressure is only half that at sea level. Thus the barometer makes a very good altimeter. Conversely, the altimeter makes a very good barometer!

Atmospheric pressure can be measured most reliably with a mercury barometer. However, an aneroid barometer is normally used on a boat. The aneroid barometer consists of a flexible metal box, usually made of beryllium or steel, which contains a vacuum. The sides of the box are held apart by a spring against the atmospheric pressure, which would tend to make it collapse. This mechanism is connected to a pointer which indicates the atmospheric pressure on a dial.

The dial can be calibrated by reference to an accurate mercury barometer. The instrument can be adjusted by means of a screw at the back. When taking a reading from an aneroid barometer, tap the glass lightly. This will allow the pointer to shift to the right place on the dial.

When on board you should place the barometer in a shady spot. And when you store the boat away for the winter, take the barometer home with you.

Most barometer dials include information about the weather to expect for different readings (sunny, changeable, rain). Such 'information' is quite unsuitable for weather forecasting and should be ignored. However, it is most important to measure any **change** in pressure. This is known as the **tendency** and may be stable, rising or falling. For reading this it is essential to use the second pointer regularly. This pointer is simply moved by hand. It can be matched

The precision barometer.

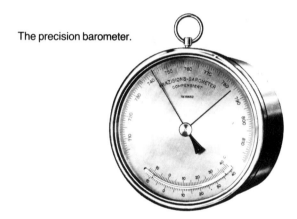

A combination of instruments: thermometer, barometer and hygrometer.

The cup anemometer.

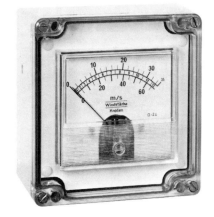

The wind-speed dial. Electrical impulses are received from the anemometer.

with the first pointer so that any subsequent change in pressure can be measured. The more unsettled the weather is, the more essential it is to measure the atmospheric pressure at short intervals.

Mercury barometers have become very rare on ships these days. They are never to be recommended for sailing vessels, being difficult to install and awkward to read.

If you want to measure the atmospheric pressure continuously, a **barograph** is the instrument to use. A barograph consists of an aneroid barometer which measures the pressure continuously. It draws a trace on a strip of paper on a slowly rotating drum. Especially when embarking on a longer trip, you will need a more accurate means of weather forecasting. The shape of the line on the barograph will assist you in this. Gentle curves indicate calm weather; violent zig-zags are a warning of unstable conditions. The movement of the ship can pose a problem by distorting the line on the barograph. More expensive instruments have damping mechanisms. The sensitive plotter can also be affected by engine vibrations in a motor boat, but this can be lessened by the use of insulating panels.

Atmospheric pressure shows noticeable daily variations, such as a rising tendency in the morning and at midnight. A fall in pressure in the afternoon is particularly marked in the summer as a result of warming. These daily variations amount to an average of 1 mbar in Europe. They are greater over tropical waters, where they can be as much as 4 mbar. Changes in pressure should therefore be particularly noted when they are different from the daily pattern.

Atmospheric pressure has also been shown to go through regular yearly cycles. These depend upon the distribution of land and sea and in the way they are warmed. These cycles combine with the general weather patterns across the globe.

Variations in air pressure are shown on weather maps by the use of **isobars**. These are lines which connect points of equal atmospheric pressure. On most weather maps isobars are drawn at 5 mbar intervals. The **high-pressure area** or **high** is surrounded by isobars of lower pressures. The **low-pressure area** or **low** is surrounded by isobars of rising pressure.

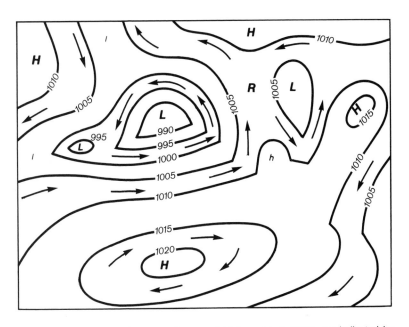

A section from a weather map. Low- and high-pressure areas are indicated by isobars. The arrows show wind directions. The isobars are drawn at 5-mbar intervals. The air circulates in a clockwise direction round a high and in an anticlockwise direction round a low. This is due to the rotation of the earth (the Coriolis effect). The earth's rotation also affects the duration period of highs and lows.
H = high, L = low, R = ridge of high pressure, h = wedge of high pressure, l = trough of low pressure.

The distances between the isobars are of particular interest to the sailor. These distances are an indication of the speed with which the pressure falls, known as the pressure gradient:

Distance between isobars	Pressure difference	Weather conditions
small	great	stormy
great	small	calm

The pressure gradient can be calculated as follows. First measure the pressure difference along a line 60 nautical miles (111 km) in length at right angles to the isobars. Suppose that there are two isobars measuring 1,005 mbar and 1,010 mbar respectively, and 50 nautical miles apart. The calculation will run thus (x being the pressure gradient required):

$$x = (1,010 - 1,005)/50 = 0.1 \text{ mbar per nautical mile.}$$

Therefore the pressure difference over the 60 nautical miles is $60 \times 0.1 = 6$ mbar.

Wind

This is a very important section for both sailors and windsurfers. Some general points: wind is simply the movement of air. It occurs when air moves from an area of high pressure to an area of low pressure. It is characterised both by its strength and by its direction.

Wind direction
Wind direction is normally understood to be the direction *from* which the wind is blowing. For example, the west wind blows from west to east.

The wind-rose indicates wind direction more exactly in degrees. Starting from north it moves clockwise through east (90°), south (180°), west (270°) and back to north (360°). Meteorologists use this system. Sailors often continue to use the traditional divisions (north, east by north, north-north-east, north by north-east, etc.). Each such division is equivalent to 11.25° (11° 15′).

The wind-rose shows the wind directions in degrees from north, through east, to south and west. The wind direction means the direction from which the air current is moving. The west wind blows from west to east.

Wind strength

Wind strength is normally given as the wind speed measured at a specific time. This may be measured in several ways:

- In nautical miles per hour (knots),
- In miles per hour (mph),
- In metres per second (m/s),
- In kilometres per hour (km/h).

The relationship between m/s and knots is expressed thus (to a good approximation):

m/s × 2 = knots

The wind force indicated on the Beaufort Scale is vitally important for sailing. It is given in numbers from force 0 to force 12.

17

Beaufort Scale and wind speed
(The international standard since 1949)

Beaufort No.	Designation	Effects of the wind inland
0	calm	No wind; smoke rises vertically.
1	light air	Wind direction indicated by smoke drift, but not by wind vanes.
2	light breeze	Wind felt on face; leaves rustle; wind vanes moved by wind.
3	gentle breeze	Leaves and twigs in constant motion; wind extends a light flag.
4	moderate breeze	Raises dust and loose paper; small branches are moved
5	fresh breeze	Small trees in leaf begin to sway; crested wavelets form on inland waters.
6	strong breeze	Large branches in motion; whistling in telegraph wires; umbrellas difficult to use.
7	moderate gale	Whole trees in motion; difficulty felt when walking against the wind.
8	gale	Twigs broken from trees; progress considerably impeded when walking.
9	severe gale	Slight structural damage (chimney pots and tiles removed).
10	storm	Trees uprooted; considerable structural damage.
11	severe storm	Widespread damage (rarely experienced inland).
12	hurricane	Total devastation (virtually unknown inland).

Beaufort Number	Effects of the wind on the sea	Wind Speeds (m/s)	Average Speed (knots)	Weather Map Symbol
0	Smooth, glassy sea.	0– 0.2	under 1	
1	Small, scale-like ripples without crests.	0.3– 1.5	2	
2	Small waves, still short and smooth, but more pronounced.	1.6– 3.3	5	
3	White caps forming, but still mostly smooth. Occasional appearance of white foam.	3.4– 5.4	8	
4	Waves still small, but longer. White caps now fairly general.	5.5– 7.9	13	
5	Moderate-sized waves, now long and more pronounced. White caps everywhere. Occasional formation of spray	8.0–10.7	18	
6	Formation of larger waves. Wave crests break and leave areas of white foam. Some spray.	10.8–13.8	24	
7	Sea heaps up. Long streaks of foam begin to form along the direction of the wind. More spray.	13.9–17.1	30	
8	Large waves with very long crests. Spray blown off the wave crests. Long, thick streaks of foam.	17.2–20.7	37	
9	Mountainous seas. Dense streaks of foam along the direction of the wind. Crests of waves begin to topple and roll over. Spray may affect visibility.	20.8–24.4	44	
10	Towering waves with long overhanging crests. Sea white with foam. The tumbling of sea becomes heavy and shock-like. Visibility affected.	24.5–28.4	52	
11	Extremely mountainous seas. Sea white and frothy. Visibility considerably reduced by spray.	28.5–32.6	60	
12	Air completely filled with foam and spray. Sea white and frothy with driving spray. Visibility seriously reduced.	32.7–36.9	68	

It is very helpful if you can judge the wind strength for yourself. This is possible if you know the effects on land and sea of winds of different forces on the Beaufort Scale. Some indication of this is given in the tables on pages 18 and 19. There are further illustrations on pages 22 onwards, which show the sea conditions at different wind strengths. Estimated Beaufort numbers are provided for each picture.

If you want to measure the wind speed afloat the **cup anemometer** is the instrument to use (see page 14). The dial of this instrument is usually calibrated in metres per second (m/s). It can either be a hand gadget (a **ventimeter**) or take the form of a remote indicating instrument. The remote indicator is very expensive, but it can be mounted in a more favourable position, such as the top of the mast. When using a ventimeter, be careful to place it in a spot where there is no turbulence. Parts of the boat such as the cabin can interfere with the measurement of the wind.

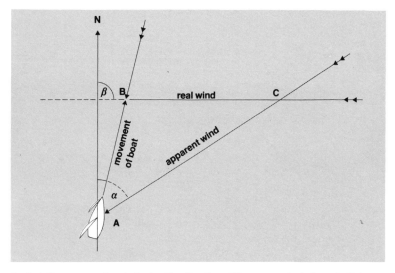

A wind diagram: angle α indicates the direction of the apparent wind; angle β shows the direction of the real wind.

Observation of the wind

It is not easy to find a suitable position on a boat for mounting an anemometer. That apart, it is no simple task to observe the wind direction from a moving boat. For this it is essential to distinguish between the apparent wind and the real wind.

The apparent wind is produced by a combination of the real wind and the speed of the boat. If it were calm, for example, any movement of the boat would produce an apparent wind from the opposite direction. The wind diagram on the previous page gives an example. Suppose that our boat is travelling in a straight line in a direction of 14° at a speed of 9 knots. From observation we calculate an apparent wind of 16 knots from the direction east-north-east (57°). The lines of the wind triangle can be drawn accordingly: the line AB gives the course of the boat, its length representing its speed of 9 knots; the line CA represents the speed and direction of the apparent wind. The direction and strength of the real wind is represented by the line connecting points C and B — 11.25 knots from due east.

When making observations about the wind, note the following:

1. The movement of clouds does not give a valid indication of wind speed and direction. You must know about the surface wind, and not about the winds higher up.
2. The wind speed undergoes much more marked variations than the wind direction. The wind over lakes is strongly affected by the surrounding terrain, especially in mountainous regions. Areas of turbulence often occur on the water surface.
3. The apparent wind hauls forward as the boat accelerates. The apparent wind always blows more on the bows than the real wind.
4. When estimating the real wind over the sea, observation of the wind waves is always helpful. Note the wave directions, and the formation of spindrift from breaking waves.
5. A change in the wind is not immediately followed by a change in the waves.
6. The wind **veers** when it turns in a **clockwise** direction. A south-westerly gale veers westerly. The wind **backs** when it turns in an **anticlockwise** direction. A south-easterly gale backs easterly.

The strength of the apparent wind is a decisive factor in the propulsion of a sailing vessel. Continual observation of the wind is vital for any sailor, whether on the lakes or on the sea. Extra care is required when sailing along coasts or on the open sea. You must note down all changes of wind speed or direction in the log-book, together with times of observation. You should also make a regular hourly entry in the log-book, including all wind details.

Force 0 (calm). Remains of a slight swell in the picture.

Force 1 (light air). Ripples without crests.

Force 2 (slight breeze). Small waves which do not break.

Force 3 (gentle breeze). Waves gradually beginning to break.

Force 4 (moderate breeze). White caps appear. Waves longer.

Force 5 (fresh breeze). White caps everywhere. Waves still longer.

Force 6 (strong breeze). Waves breaking into white areas of foam. Large waves forming.

Force 7 (moderate gale). Formation of long streaks of foam along the direction of the wind.

Force 8 (gale). Formation of long, thick streaks of foam. Spray blown from wave crests.

Force 9 (severe gale). Visibility affected by spray. Wave crests begin to topple and roll over.

Force 10 (storm). Large areas of foam. Towering waves with long overhanging crests. Spray hinders visibility.

Force 11 (severe storm). Everywhere wave crests explode into spray. Exceptionally high waves. Visibility considerably reduced.

Force 12 (hurricane). Air filled with foam and spray. Sea white with driving spray. Visibility completely reduced.

Swell. A trawler in a heavy swell with light winds.

A cross-sea. Gale-force winds. High cross-sea in the centre of the picture.

Breakers on a sea wall on the island of Norderney.

Surf off the island of Sylt.

Surface boundary between two different water masses.

Whirlpool in a strong tidal current.

In weather reports there is a special scale for indicating wind directions. This scale has 36 divisions, each of 10°. '00' indicates calm. The eight primary directions are as follows:

```
05 =  50° = north-easterly wind (NE)
09 =  90° = easterly wind (E)
14 = 140° = south-easterly wind (SE)
18 = 180° = southerly wind (S)
23 = 230° = south-westerly wind (SW)
27 = 270° = westerly wind (W)
32 = 320° = north-westerly wind (NW)
36 = 360° = northerly wind (N)
```

There are a further 28 divisions, which are described as follows:

8 secondary directions:
02 = NNE, 07 = ENE, 11 = ESE, 16 = SSE, 20 = SSW,
25 = WSW, 29 = WNW, 34 = NNW.

20 tertiary directions, distributed among the remaining divisions:
01, 03, 04, 06, 08 in the north-eastern sector;
10, 12, 13, 15, 17 in the south-eastern sector;
19, 21, 22, 24, 26 in the south-western sector;
28, 30, 31, 33, 35 in the north-western sector.

It would be wrong to conclude from this that the wind usually blows from the primary directions. After all, the wind 'blows where it wills'. In Western Europe the wind blows mostly from westerly points (between 23 and 32). In the northern trade-wind zones there is a predominance of north-easterlies (between 03 and 07).

Wind arrows on weather maps
Meteorologists use wind arrows to indicate wind speeds and directions at observation stations. The arrows are drawn so as to indicate the direction from which the wind is blowing onto the weather station.

Wind speeds are shown by barbs at the ends of the arrows. A whole barb corresponds to 2 divisions on the Beaufort Scale, a half-barb to 1 division. For reasons of simplicity, storm force 10 is shown in the form of a black triangle. The barbs are always drawn on the arrows in the direction of low pressure.

If the weather station is shown as a double circle on the weather map, this means that there is no wind at all at the time of observation. All these wind symbols are shown in the chart on page 19.

In order to give the average wind conditions for a particular area, a **wind-rose** is used. The example diagram below gives information in the following manner.

Number in circle = Number of calm days observed.
Length of arrows = Relative frequency of each wind direction
Number of barbs = Average wind speed on the Beaufort Scale.

Statistical averages such as are given in monthly summaries can only serve as an approximate guide. The weather conditions can be totally different at any given time.

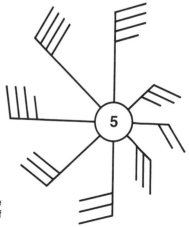

A wind-rose. This is used to show the average wind conditions in the course of a month in a particular area.

The state of the sea

Whenever you are afloat you must pay attention to the wave conditions. The state of the water surface is known in technical terms as the **sea state** or the **state of the sea**. The sea state gives us information about the effect of the wind on the water surface. This may be directly in the form of **wind waves** or indirectly in the form of **swell**. Waves of varying dimensions will be produced. The study of the sea state involves primarily the observation of the waves.

On the open sea, the wind waves are the result of local wind conditions. The characteristics of wind waves depend on

- the strength of the wind,
- the duration of the wind,
- the fetch of the wind.

The fetch of the wind is the length of the stretch of water affected by the wind. To produce wind waves to maximum effect, the wind must have a large area of sea to work upon. The wind speed alone is not sufficient. Strong winds require a long fetch for the full development of wind waves, and the only 'ideal' place for this is the open sea. Inland lakes and coasts are affected by local differences. The effect of a breakwater in keeping a harbour calm in the roughest of storms is an illustration of this. The behaviour of the wind itself can also be affected by local topography and general weather conditions (for turbulence see page 61).

Even in so-called ideal conditions the wind waves are mostly irregular, being of variable size and frequency. Waves can be measured according to the following criteria:

- wave height,
- wave length,
- wave period (or frequency).

You should always try to work out the wave dimensions, although given their variability this is no simple task. The tables on page 34 may be of assistance in this. The first is the *Nautical Sea Scale*, which links the state of the sea to the Beaufort Scale. The second table shows the sea and swell scale laid down by the *World Meteorological Organisation*, which gives corresponding wave heights.

The third table gives information on the dimensions of storm waves encountered in different sea areas. The longest and highest waves to be observed have been in the South Atlantic, where waves have been known to reach heights of 20 m (65 ft) and lengths of 800 m (½ mile).

Nautical sea scale

Wind force	Sea state	Wind force	Sea state
0	0 calm (glassy)	6	5 very rough
1	1 smooth (rippled)	7	6 high
2/3	2 slight	8/9	7 very high
4	3 moderate	10	8 precipitous
5	4 rough	11/12	9 confused

Sea and swell scale

Description of the sea state Wind waves	Swell	Characteristic wave heights
0 calm	no swell	0
1 smooth	low swell (short/average length)	0–0.1 m (0.3 ft)
2 slight	low swell (long)	0.1–0.5 m (1.5 ft)
3 moderate	moderate swell (short)	0.5–1.25 m (4 ft)
4 rough	moderate swell (average length)	1.25–2.5 m (8 ft)
5 very rough	moderate swell (long)	2.5–4 m (13 ft)
6 high	heavy swell (short)	4–6 m (20 ft)
7 very high	heavy swell (average length)	6–9 m (30 ft)
8 precipitous	heavy swell (long)	9–14 m (46 ft)
9 confused	confused	over 14m (over 46 ft)

Storm waves

Sea area	Wave heights	Wave lengths	Wave period	Wave speeds
Western Baltic	3 m (10 ft)	55–70 m (180–230 ft)	6–7 s	9–10 m/s (18–20 kn)
Southern North Sea	6 m (20 ft)	120 m (400 ft)	10 s	12 m/s (24 kn)
Northern North Sea	8–9 m (25–30 ft)	180–200 m (600–660 ft)	11–12 s	16–17 m/s (32–34 kn)
North Atlantic (west-wind zone)	16–18 m (50–60 ft)	250 m (830 ft)	13 s	20 m/s (40 kn)

Swell is the term used for those waves produced by winds elsewhere, or by winds which have already abated. Waves extend further and take longer to dissipate than the winds which produce them. Swell waves are usually shallower but longer than wind waves. Wave systems from different directions are often superimposed upon one another, producing what is known as a **cross-sea**. A cross-sea is often produced when wind waves cross a well-established swell. The interference patterns will produce unusually high waves, which pose a danger to shipping.

Sailing in coastal waters is affected by **breakers**. These are produced in shallow waters, and are influenced by local factors, including

- the shape of the sea-bed, in particular its steepness;
- the shape of the coast;
- the depth of the water;
- the direction of the wind.

It is particularly important to know how deep-water waves behave when they enter the shallows. Friction with the sea-bed makes the waves steeper and encourages them to break more frequently. This phenomenon is especially marked in the North Sea, where the relative shallowness and the variable depth of the sea accentuate the development of breakers. A northerly or north-easterly gale can, for example, produce enormous breakers over the Dogger and Fisher Banks, which will pose considerable dangers for small boats.

When sailing in coastal waters, note the following:

1. Long waves become considerably higher near the shore.
2. Waves change direction as they approach shelving coastlines. They eventually become parallel to the coast. This can produce waves of variable heights.
3. Waves are thrown back by steep coasts and cliffs. These reflected waves are superimposed on approaching waves, producing a very choppy sea.
4. Cross-seas form round islands and headlands. Waves are deflected from both sides, producing interference patterns. The waters round Land's End and the Scilly Isles are notorious for this.
5. Standing waves (regular waves) form in harbours.

Breakers take different forms on coasts and shallows. There are the violent breakers which form on cliffs and rocks, accompanied by foam and spray. On wide, shallow beaches the breakers take the form of surf. The water from the surf streams back to form more breakers. Strong currents can develop in the shallows, most of which are in the direction of the open sea.

Breakers tower up suddenly and then break. Windsurfers should approach them at full speed and meet them head-on.

Here are a few general observations on the state of the sea which every sailor should know:

1. A wind off the land produces smaller waves than a wind off the sea.
2. If the water area is small the wind waves are never fully developed.
3. The smaller the lake, the smaller the waves.
4. The swell on the open sea is relatively harmless, but can use up a lot of power and slow down the journey.
5. High wind waves and a heavy swell from different directions can produce a dangerous cross-sea.
6. High wind waves produce a lot of breakers, which can be dangerous to boats.
7. Cold winds produce higher waves than warm winds of the same strength. Damp winds are often gusty, and produce particularly choppy seas.

8. A tidal current running against the wind waves will produce slower but steeper waves.
9. A severe storm over the sea will produce a heavy swell which will travel a long way ahead of it.
10. Breakers can reach heights of 15 m (50 ft) and more.

A sailor must rely mostly on visual observation of the state of the sea. But waves can be measured instrumentally for the purposes of meteorological and hydrological research. The sea state can be assessed by the measurement of water pressures. Waves can be measured on board ship, using echo-sounders to measure wave heights and radar to measure wave lengths. Photography from ships and aeroplanes is also valuable in the scientific observation of waves.

Temperature

We now come to an important element of all weather observations. The behaviour of warm and cold air masses must be considered in every weather forecast. By air temperature we mean the temperature of the air near the surface of the land or water. After temperature, the next most important measurement is humidity, or the amount of water vapour present in the air. This is dealt with on page 39.

The air temperature is measured with a **thermometer**. This instrument can be either a liquid or a bimetal thermometer. The latter is sometimes fitted with an adjustment screw. The liquid thermometer functions on the basis that the liquid expands when warmed and contracts when cooled. The bimetal thermometer consists of two strips of metal welded together. The metals have different thermal expansion rates and bend with heat. The temperature can be measured from the degree of deflection. Maximum and minimum thermometers are especially useful instruments. They can record the highest and lowest temperatures recorded in the daily temperature cycle.

The reference points for the calibration of liquid thermometers are the freezing and boiling points of water under specified conditions. The mercury or alcohol contained in the thermometer will reach different levels on the scale between or outside these two points. The scale is divided into equal degrees in one (or two) of the three scales which are used. Of these three scales the Celsius or Centigrade scale has been adopted as the international standard. Here are comparative tables showing the correspondences between the three scales.

Comparative tables of the thermometer scales

Celsius (Centigrade)	Fahrenheit	Réaumur
–25°	–13°	–20°
–15°	+ 5°	–12°
– 5°	+23°	– 4°
0°	+32°	0°
+ 5°	+41°	+ 4°
+10°	+50°	+ 8°
+15°	+59°	+12°
+20°	+68°	+16°
+25°	+77°	+20°
+30°	+86°	+24°
+35°	+95°	+28°
+40°	+104°	+32°

Fixed points on the thermometer scales

	Celsius	Fahrenheit	Réaumur
Freezing point	0°	+ 32°	0°
Boiling point	+100°	+212°	+80°

A very rough guide for converting Celsius to Fahrenheit: multiply by 2 and add 30 (e.g. 10°C = 2 × 10 + 30 = 50°F).

To measure the true air temperature the thermometer must be protected from direct sunlight and from reservoirs of heat. The cabin is far from the ideal place for measuring the air temperature. The thermometer must be well ventilated, and for this reason the windward side of the boat is to be recommended. You should, however, be careful to keep the instrument dry. Any water from splashing or spray will evaporate from the thermometer bulb, thus absorbing heat from it.

The whirling or sling thermometer is particularly suited for use on a boat. It is indispensable for sea and coastal sailing. Exact temperature measurements are necessary for this purpose, preferably to tenths of a degree. They are required in order to observe the exchange of heat between the water surface and the nearby air. You must also measure the water temperature accurately. There is a special water thermometer for this purpose. This measurement can also be distorted if the instrument is warmed by the boat. The water thermometer should be protected from wind as well as sun.

Fixed thermometers are not to be recommended on board. For this reason sailors have no use for a thermograph (an instrument for measuring temperature continuously).

The air temperature undergoes daily variations. This is less noticeable over water than on land, and less still over the open sea, owing to the different warming rates of land and water. Daily variations over land amount to approximately $5 - 10C°$ provided that the solar radiation is uninterrupted. The minimum occurs just before sunrise and the maximum in the early afternoon. Over the open sea the variation amounts to only one or two degrees. Lakes are more strongly influenced by the surrounding land.

Temperatures also go through a yearly cycle. In Western Europe the lowest temperatures normally occur at the end of January and the highest at the end of July. This corresponds to four weeks after the winter and summer equinoxes. Again there is a difference between land and sea. The sea warms more slowly and less markedly. Hence we speak of maritime climates, with cool summers and mild winters, as against continental climates, with hot summers and cold winters. This difference also applies, to a limited extent, to large inland lakes such as Lake Geneva and Lake Constance. Their influence is felt particularly in the autumn, when they cool down more gradually than the surrounding land.

If there is a change in temperature which is noticeably different from the normal daily cycle, this is a sign of a change in the weather.

Humidity and condensation

The moisture content of the air is extremely important for the weather. Everyone can tell the difference between damp air and dry air. The degree of humidity is determined by the amount of invisible water vapour contained in the air. Water vapour is water in the form of gas, which has entered the atmosphere through evaporation. Heat is absorbed in this process. It is known as latent heat and is preserved in the water vapour. When the water vapour condenses this latent heat is released again. Thus energy is transformed and transported over considerable distances. This physical process is vital to weather, as we shall discover later.

The humidity is defined as the amount of water vapour (expressed in grams) contained in one cubic metre of air. How much water vapour can the air absorb? The amount is limited and depends upon the air temperature. In the summer there can be as much as 30 grams per cubic metre of air. At freezing point the air can scarcely hold as much as 5 grams per cubic metre (g/m³).

The maximum humidity possible at a particular temperature is known as the **saturation humidity**. This can be tabulated as follows:

4.8 g/m³ at 0°C	17.3 g/m³ at 20°C
9.4 g/m³ at 10°C	30.4 g/m³ at 30°C

The actual humidity of the air is known as the **absolute humidity**. This can be less than, but never more than, the saturation humidity for that particular temperature. The **relative humidity** is the actual humidity expressed as a percentage of the saturation humidity. When a weather reporter talks of 63% humidity, he is speaking of the relative humidity of the air. This can be expressed as a formula:

$$\text{Relative humidity} = \frac{\text{Absolute humidity}}{\text{Saturation humidity}} \times 100\%$$

Here is an example: the temperature is 20°C and the absolute humidity 10 g/m³. The saturation humidity is 17.3 g/m³ (see table above). We then calculate as follows:

$$\text{Relative humidity} = \frac{10 \times 100\%}{17.3} = 58\%$$

If the temperature rises, the relative humidity will fall; if the temperature falls, the relative humidity will rise. In other words:

When air is warmed it becomes drier.
When air is cooled it becomes damper.

If the temperature falls to 10°C the air can no longer hold any more than 9.4 g/m³ water vapour. If this happens in our example, 0.6 g/m³ water vapour must be released in liquid form as water droplets. This process is known as **condensation**. The temperature at which condensation begins is known as the **dewpoint temperature**.

Although water vapour is only present in small amounts in the air, the amount of liquid water present in a cloud can be considerable. In a thunder-cloud there can be more than 100,000 tons of water.

Humidity can be measured with either a **hygrometer** or a **psychrometer**. These instruments give the relative humidity. The hygrometer makes use of a human hair, which becomes longer as it becomes moist. The psychrometer consists of two identical thermometers, one of which is kept dry and the other wet. The relative humidity can be ascertained by measuring the temperature difference between the two thermometers. In order to do this a humidity table is required (see page 42). Once the temperature and the temperature difference between the thermometers is known, the relative humidity can be read from the table.

The whirling or sling psychrometer is normally used on a boat. It is comparable to the whirling thermometer, but consists of two thermometers, one of which is wrapped in moist fabric.

Condensation can take many forms. Above freezing point the water vapour changes into liquid form as it reaches the dewpoint. Water droplets are formed as dew on the ground, and as cloud or fog in the air. Below freezing point the water vapour freezes directly into frost on the ground, and into ice crystals in the air. Ice crystals can also change directly into water vapour. This is known as sublimation. For condensation to occur, condensation nuclei are required. These are particles of dust and smoke which are present in the air, and round which the water droplets form.

Fog over the sea.

Table for determining relative humidity and dewpoint

Difference between the temperatures on the dry and wet thermometers in Centigrade degrees

t	0		1			2			3			4			5			6			7			8			9			10		
	e	f	a	r	T	a	r	T	a	r	T	a	r	T	a	r	T	a	r	T	a	r	T	a	r	T	a	r	T	a	r	T
−15	1.4	1.6	0.7	57	22	0.8	38	22																									
−10	2.1	2.4	1.4	69	15	1.1	42	20																									
−9	2.3	2.5	1.6	71	13	1.3	45	18																									
−8	2.5	2.7	1.8	73	12	1.5	49	16																									
−7	2.7	3.0	1.9	74	11	1.6	52	14	0.7	24	25																						
−6	2.9	3.2	2.2	75	10	1.8	54	13	0.9	28	22																						
−5	3.2	3.4	2.4	77	8	2.0	57	11	1.0	32	19																						
−4	3.4	3.7	2.6	78	7	2.1	59	10	1.2	36	17	0.5	15	28																			
−3	3.7	3.9	2.8	79	6	2.4	61	8	1.4	39	15	0.8	19	24																			
−2	4.0	4.2	3.1	80	5	2.7	63	7	1.6	42	13	1.0	23	20																			
−1	4.3	4.5	3.4	81	4	2.9	64	6	1.8	45	11	1.2	27	17																			
0	4.6	4.8	3.7	82	3	3.2	66	4	2.1	47	9	1.4	31	15	0.6	14	24																
+1	4.9	5.2	4.1	83	−1	3.6	68	3	2.4	50	8	1.6	34	12	0.9	18	20																
+2	5.3	5.6	4.4	84	0	3.9	69	2	2.7	52	6	1.9	37	11	1.1	22	17																
+3	5.7	6.0	4.8	84	+1	4.3	70	−1	3.1	54	5	2.2	40	9	1.4	25	14	0.7	12	23													
+4	6.1	6.4	5.2	85	2	4.7	72	0	3.4	56	4	2.6	42	7	1.7	28	12	1.0	16	19													
+5	6.5	6.8	5.6	86	3	5.1	73	+1	3.8	58	2	2.9	45	5	2.1	32	9	1.2	19	15	0.5	7	27										
+6	7.0	7.3	6.0	86	4	5.5	75	3	4.2	60	−1	3.3	47	4	2.4	35	8	1.6	23	13	0.8	11	21										
+7	7.5	7.8	6.5	87	5	6.0	75	4	4.6	61	0	3.7	49	3	2.8	37	6	1.9	26	10	1.1	14	17										
+8	8.0	8.3	7.0	87	6	6.5	76	5	5.0	62	+1	4.1	51	−1	3.2	40	4	2.3	29	8	1.4	18	14	0.6	7	23							
+9	8.6	8.8	7.5	88	7				5.5	64	3	4.5	53	0	3.6	42	3	2.7	31	7	1.8	21	11	0.9	11	18							

Temperature of the dry thermometer in Centigrade degrees — t

e is the maximum vapour pressure in mm Hg at the temperature t.
f is the saturation humidity over water in g/m³ at the temperature t.
a is the absolute humidity in g/m³ at the temperature t.
r is the relative humidity in % at the temperature t.
T is the dewpoint, i.e. the temperature to which the air must be cooled to become saturated, rounded to the nearest whole degree Centigrade.
The values count for all barometer pressures between 980 and 1030 mbar.

Continuation

Temperature of the dry thermometer in Centigrade degrees	Difference between the temperatures on the dry and wet thermometers in Centigrade degrees																															
	0		1			2			3			4			5			6			7			8			9			10		
t	*e*	*f*	*a*	*r*	*T*	*a*	*r*	*T*	*a*	*r*	*T*	*a*	*r*	*T*	*a*	*r*	*T*	*a*	*r*	*T*	*a*	*r*	*T*	*a*	*r*	*T*	*a*	*r*	*T*	*a*	*r*	*T*
+10	9.2	9.4	8.1	88	8	7.0	77	6	6.0	65	4	5.0	55	+1	4.0	44	−2	3.1	34	5	2.2	24	9	1.3	14	9	0.4	5	26			
+11	9.8	10.0	8.7	88	9	7.6	77	7	6.5	66	5	5.5	56	3	4.5	46	0	3.5	36	3	2.6	26	7	1.7	17	12	0.8	8	26			
+12	10.5	10.7	9.3	89	10	8.1	78	8	7.1	68	6	6.0	57	4	5.0	48	+1	4.0	38	−2	3.0	29	5	2.1	20	9	1.2	11	16			
+13	11.2	11.4	10.0	89	11	8.8	79	9	7.7	69	7	6.6	59	5	5.5	49	3	4.5	40	0	3.5	31	3	2.5	23	7	1.6	14	12	0.7	6	22
+14	12.0	12.1	10.7	90	12	9.5	79	11	8.3	70	9	7.2	60	6	6.1	51	4	5.0	42	+1	4.0	33	−2	3.0	25	5	2.0	17	10	1.1	9	17
+15	12.8	12.9	11.4	90	13	10.1	80	12	9.0	71	10	7.8	61	8	6.7	53	5	5.6	44	3	4.5	35	0	3.5	27	3	2.5	20	7	1.5	12	13
+16	13.6	13.7	12.2	90	14	10.9	81	13	9.7	71	11	8.5	62	9	7.3	54	7	6.2	46	4	5.1	37	+2	4.0	30	−2	3.0	22	5	2.0	15	10
+17	14.5	14.5	13.1	90	15	11.7	81	14	10.4	72	12	9.2	63	10	8.0	55	8	6.8	47	6	5.7	39	3	4.6	32	0	3.5	24	3	2.5	17	7
+18	15.5	15.4	14.0	91	16	12.6	82	15	11.2	73	13	9.9	65	11	8.7	56	9	7.5	49	7	6.3	41	5	5.2	34	+2	4.1	27	−1	3.0	20	5
+19	16.5	16.3	14.9	91	17	13.4	82	16	12.1	74	14	10.7	65	12	9.4	58	10	8.2	50	8	7.0	43	6	5.8	36	3	4.7	29	0	3.6	22	3
+20	17.5	17.3	15.9	91	19	14.4	83	17	13.0	74	15	11.6	66	14	10.2	59	12	8.9	51	10	7.7	44	7	6.5	37	5	5.3	31	+2	4.2	24	−1
+21	18.7	18.4	16.9	91	20	15.4	83	18	13.9	75	16	12.4	67	15	11.1	60	13	9.7	52	11	8.4	45	9	7.2	39	6	6.0	32	4	4.8	26	+1
+22	19.8	19.4	18.0	92	21	16.4	83	19	14.9	75	18	13.4	68	16	12.0	61	14	10.6	54	12	9.2	47	10	7.9	40	8	6.7	34	5	5.5	28	3
+23	21.1	20.6	19.2	92	22	17.5	84	20	15.9	76	19	14.4	69	17	12.9	62	15	11.4	55	13	10.1	48	11	8.7	42	9	7.4	36	7	6.2	30	4
+24	22.4	21.8	20.4	92	23	18.7	84	21	17.0	77	20	15.4	70	18	13.9	62	16	12.4	56	15	11.0	49	13	9.6	43	11	8.2	37	8	6.9	31	6
+25	23.8	23.1	21.7	92	24	19.9	85	22	18.2	77	21	16.5	70	19	14.9	63	18	13.4	57	16	11.9	51	14	10.4	44	12	9.1	39	10	7.7	33	7
+26	25.2	24.4	23.0	92	25	21.2	85	23	19.4	78	22	17.7	71	20	16.0	64	19	14.4	58	17	12.9	51	15	11.4	45	13	9.9	40	11	8.6	34	9
+27	26.7	25.8	24.5	93	26	22.5	85	24	20.7	78	23	18.9	71	21	17.2	65	20	15.5	59	18	13.9	53	16	12.4	47	15	10.9	41	13	9.4	36	10
+28	28.3	27.2	26.0	93	27	24.0	86	25	22.0	79	24	20.2	72	22	18.4	65	21	16.7	59	19	15.0	53	18	13.4	48	16	11.9	42	14	10.4	37	12
+29	30.0	28.8	27.6	93	28	25.5	86	26	23.5	79	25	21.6	72	24	19.7	66	22	17.9	60	20	16.2	54	19	14.5	49	17	12.9	43	15	11.4	38	13
+30	31.8	30.4	29.3	93	29	27.1	86	27	25.0	79	26	23.0	73	25	21.0	67	23	19.2	61	22	17.4	55	20	15.7	50	18	14.0	44	16	12.4	39	15

Haze

Although haze does not constitute a form of condensation, it is important because it is a precursor of condensation. As haze is normally associated with loss of visibility it is worthy of the sailor's attention. The problems of visibility and related circumstances are dealt with on page 56.

Haze develops as water vapour molecules become attached to condensation nuclei. The water vapour is approaching the dewpoint, but has not yet reached it.

There are forms of haze which are entirely attributable to the density of smoke, sand or dust in the air. This can be caused by desert winds or forest fires.

Lastly, haze can build up over the sea as a result of high waves or breakers.

Mist and fog

This form of condensation is rightly feared by sailors. Whether over the open sea, in coastal waters, or on lakes and rivers, fog can constitute a dangerous hindrance to navigation. Fog is by no means confined to particular times of year such as November.

If the visibility drops below 1,000 m, this is defined as being a type of fog. Fog is just like a cloud, consisting of a large collection of water droplets.

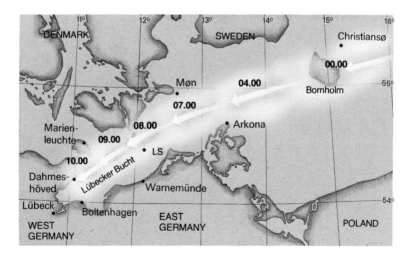

Sea fog in the Lübecker Bucht, July 1978.

How does fog develop? Three elements are required for this: water vapour, condensation nuclei, and a drop in temperature. In practice several types of fog development can be distinguished:

1. **Cooling fog:** warm air masses are cooled by a cooler water surface.
2. **Advection fog:** cool air mixes with warmer, more humid air.
3. **Evaporation fog:** cold air passes over a warmer water surface. Evaporation causes the cold air to become moister.
4. **Radiation fog:** on a clear night, the ground and the nearby air cool rapidly until the temperature reaches the dewpoint.

Cooling fogs

Cooling fogs normally develop over the sea, and are therefore often known as sea fogs. They are frequently dense and persistent, extending over large areas. Cooling fogs can be particularly dense when they form over cold sea currents.

As the sea is much cooler than the air in the spring and early summer, cooling fogs are much more frequent at this time of year. Fog is commonest in June over the North Sea (the 'sea fret'), and in April and May over the Baltic. Further north, in the seas around Iceland, July and August are the foggiest months.

Although fogs are infrequent in some months of the year, you must always be prepared for surprises. For example, summer fogs are very rare in the Lübecker Bucht. While February and March have an average of nine foggy days apiece, July and August have an average of only one day of fog. It was therefore a nasty surprise when a thick fog suddenly enveloped hundreds of sailors in the Lübecker Bucht on 30 July 1978. This event was reported by H. Schmidt in *Der Wetterlotse* ('The Weather Pilot'), pointing out the particular dangers for sailors: 'Once every three or four years a thick July fog must be reckoned with in the Lübecker Bucht. The danger of this lies in the fact that the fog does not develop gradually, but appears suddenly out of nowhere' (see the map opposite).

The weather situation was determined by a high over southern Sweden and the eastern Baltic, and a low over northern France. Moist air was thus drawn from the Polish coast into the Baltic. This air came briefly to rest in the Bornholm area under the influence of high pressure. As the water temperature was below the dewpoint of the air above it, a dense sea fog quickly developed. The air then began to move again, carrying the fog into the Lübecker Bucht.

Advection fogs

These are most frequent in coastal waters. They can develop at any time of year, preferring the westerly conditions frequent in our cool temperate latitudes. Inland, advection fogs take the form of low cloud and hill fog, and can develop in cool, windy weather.

Evaporation fogs

This form normally occurs on lakes and rivers, being most frequent in the autumn, winter and early spring. It usually develops at nightfall, lasting through into the morning.

Radiation fogs

These fogs develop over land, but can be driven by light breezes over lakes, rivers and coastal waters. They also occur mostly in the period between October and April.

Clouds

Clouds begin to form as the air cools down to the dewpoint. Clouds are made up of tiny water droplets which are prevented from falling by air currents and air resistance. Only when they become larger and heavier do the drops begin to fall as rain.

The cooling of air can be brought about in two chief ways:

1. At night and in the winter the air cools quickly by radiation. The result is the development of areas of layer-cloud, known as stratus clouds.
2. When air rises it becomes cooler. Most clouds develop from rising air currents. Sometimes the air is warmed, becomes lighter and begins to rise. This is known as **convection**, and results in the

In a fog ships can suddenly appear out of nowhere.

formation of heap-clouds, known as cumulus clouds. Sometimes air is forced to rise by an obstruction such as a mountain range. This is known as **advection**.

Clouds are important weather indicators. They give information about the air currents and the air conditions (warm or cold). If you observe the weather carefully you will notice the many different forms and patterns which clouds can assume. The variety is infinite. To bring some order out of chaos, clouds can be classified according to their type and the level at which they form:

Cloud heights	Cloud types
High-level clouds (above 5,000 m)	Cirrus (Ci) Cirrocumulus (Cc) Cirrostratus (Cs)
Medium-level clouds (2,000 – 5,000 m)	Altocumulus (Ac) Altostratus (As)
Low-level clouds (below 2,000 m)	Cumulus (Cu) Cumulonimbus (Cb) Stratocumulus (Sc) Stratus (St) Nimbostratus (Ns)

These are the 10 principal cloud types. All of them are illustrated on pages 48–52. They form the basic pattern for all clouds. A far greater variety of forms can be observed, but all of them can be seen as variants of the same 10 basic types.

You will no doubt have already noticed that clouds can be divided mostly into two main groups or cloud families. The first of these is that of the **cumulus** or **heap-clouds**. These form as a result of convection or advection, and are a sign of rising air currents. These are therefore mostly vertical in structure.

Stratus or **layer-clouds** are the result of interdependent processes, when warm, moist air encounters cooler air. The warm air, being lighter, glides over the cold air. The process is mostly horizontal in development, and leads to the formation of extensive blankets of cloud typical of stratus-type clouds.

Only the clouds in the troposphere are important in weather. In polar regions these clouds extend only to 8,000 m, whereas in the tropics they can rise as high as 18,000 m.

The cloud-base is usually lower over the sea than over the land. This is due to the higher humidity level of the air near the surface. For this reason there is more cloud generally over the sea, with a predominance of stratus cloud.

Cirrus (Ci).
These clouds are
often known as
mare's tails because
of their wispy,
feathery appearance.
They are made up of
ice crystals, and
belong to the
high-level clouds
(above 5 km).
The direction in which
they move can have
implications
regarding weather
development (see
page 67).

Cirrocumulus (Cc).
These tiny cumulus
clouds form in a
scale-like pattern,
giving what is known
as a mackerel sky.
They consist of ice
crystals and are
among the high-level
clouds (above 5 km).
They can precede a
variety of weather
types.

Cirrostratus (Cs). These clouds form a thin, whitish veil through which the sun shines, producing a characteristic halo effect. Made of ice crystals, they are high-level clouds (above 5 km). They often announce the approach of a warm front, and are therefore a frequent harbinger of rain.

Altostratus (As). A dense sheet of grey cloud, made up of ice and water, these belong to the medium-level clouds (2.5–7 km). They have variable significance for the weather.

Altocumulus (Ac). Similar to cirrocumulus, these clouds are lower and larger. However, they form similar wave patterns across the sky. They consist mostly of water droplets and are medium-level clouds (2.5–7 km). They are characteristic of changeable weather.

Nimbostratus (Ns). Dense, shapeless layer-clouds, they are made up of ice and water and cover a large area. They have a low, ragged cloud-base, but extend upwards into the medium-level clouds (2.5–7 km). These rain-clouds develop from altostratus, and often contain cumulus clouds within them.

Stratocumulus (Sc). Large grey rolls or banks of cloud, these are made up of water droplets and are among the low-level clouds (below 2.5 km). In spite of their broad expanse and threatening appearance, they are not normally rain-bearing.

Stratus (St). Amorphous blankets of cloud, often with wispy fragments or 'scud' near the ground. They are the lowest cloud form (below 2.5 km). They are associated with rain and drizzle, and form hill fog on higher ground.

Cumulus (Cu). These clouds have a loose, cauliflower-like structure. Made up of water droplets, they are low-level clouds (below 2.5 km), but can grow to higher levels. Small cumulus clouds are typical of fine weather.

Cumulonimbus (Cb) Enormous clouds of the cumulus type, often with a typical anvil-shaped top. The cloud-base is low (below 2.5 km), but these clouds can extend upwards to heights of 10 km or more. The 'anvil' is made up of ice crystals, and is typical of thunder-clouds. Otherwise, cumulonimbus clouds produce heavy rain or showers.

In weather observation, cloud height, cloud movement and cloud cover are all important. However, the sailor will mostly only have the opportunity to observe the cloud height and the amount of cloud cover. The cloud cover is shown on the weather map by the amount of black shading on the circle identifying the station (see the symbols on page 117):

cloudless (sunny)	6/8 = ¾ cloud cover (cloudy)
2/8 = ¼ cloud cover (fair)	7/8 = occasional gaps in the cloud
4/8 = ½ cloud cover	8/8 = complete cloud cover

It is very easy to overestimate the cloud cover near the horizon. This must be borne in mind when making observations from on board.

Clouds and weather change

It is never advisable to base a weather forecast on one single aspect of the weather, such as cloud formations. But the clouds can always be observed, and it is possible, with very little effort, to gain some important clues about what weather developments to look out for.

Here is a useful rule of thumb:

The presence of layer-cloud (stratus) is an indication of stable weather. The winds are correspondingly light. The concentrated development of heap-clouds (cumulus) is indicative of unstable conditions. You must expect gusty conditions, with thunderstorms in the summer.

Let us now look at the different cloud forms in more detail. The highest clouds are the **cirrus** forms, also known as ice clouds, because they are made up of ice crystals. They are often the first sign of an approaching warm front. If they become unusually dense or milky in appearance, this can presage a thunderstorm. This is particularly true over the lakes of the Alps, where they typically herald the approach of thunderstorm fronts from the south-west.

Typical of **cirrostratus** clouds is the so-called halo-phenomenon: a pale-coloured ring forms round the sun, reddish on the inside and violet on the outside. This halo-effect should not be confused with the corona of solar eclipses. Much has been written concerning the importance (or otherwise) of halo-phenomena. It cannot be seen as an exact indication of weather deterioration. Rather, it signals a general tendency for the weather to become less stable.

Altocumulus clouds are equally ambiguous in their significance in weather development. These medium-level clouds form extensive wave patterns across the sky, often known as a mackerel sky. They normally have little influence on the weather. However, a few.of

High winds in a föhn on the Starnberger See.

their variant forms should be noted. Sometimes they form more ragged, turretted tops rather like miniature cumulus. These are known as **altocumulus castellanus**, and form into long rows out of a clear sky. Another form, called **altocumulus floccus**, consists of tiny, wispy clouds. Both forms are short-lived, lasting from fifteen minutes to an hour. In the summer they appear in the morning and are a warning of possible thunder or shower development later in the day.

Thundery weather is associated with the development of enormous **cumulonimbus** clouds. These heap-clouds have a low cloud-base, but extend further up into the atmosphere. Frequently towering up to 10,000 m or higher, they have an anvil-shaped top formed of ice crystals.

Typical of heat thunderstorms is the formation of ripples of cloud, known as **altocumulus lenticularis**, on the lower side of the cumulonimbus. This usually occurs about half an hour before the thunderstorm breaks, and is a warning of approaching danger. This seldom happens with frontal thunderstorms.

The formation of ripples of altocumulus lenticularis should always be watched when the weather is thundery. This can also be observed in the föhn weather typical of alpine regions. It is caused by the downward flow of air. In thundery weather this is due to the displacement of air in the rising convection currents in the thundercloud.

Cumulus clouds are typical convection clouds. They begin at a low level, but sometimes extend to higher levels. In Europe most thunderstorms develop from cumulus clouds, so sailors should keep a careful watch on their behaviour. If they remain small and loosely-structured with little vertical growth, they are known as **cumulus humilis**. These are typical fair-weather clouds. They are harmless, and occur in fine, settled summer weather. Sometimes they bubble up into large cauliflower-like formations, known as **cumulus congestus**. Such clouds presage rain. They may eventually form into mountainous cumulonimbus clouds, with their typical anvil-shaped tops. One must then be ready for gusty, squally conditions with heavy rain, hail and thunder.

The underside of a cumulonimbus cloud is characterised by the formation of squalls. These are shown by irregular tongues of cloud below the cloud-base, and are a warning of sudden gusts of wind and rain. One important sub-form is the **cumulonimbus mamma**, in which the 'anvil-top' is particularly highly developed, filling the whole sky. Hanging down from the anvil cloud is a vast array of pouch-like or breast-shaped cloud formations, known as **mammae** or 'breasts'. This form is associated with hail and exceptionally heavy rain.

Precipitation

When the water droplets in a cloud reach a certain size they begin to fall towards the ground. This is known as **precipitation**. Whether they reach the ground depends on whether they are large enough. Sometimes they will evaporate in mid-air, as friction with the air causes them to become warmer. Precipitation is assisted by the process of coagulation, whereby several water droplets unite into one large raindrop. Liquid precipitation usually falls as rain. Raindrops can be several millimetres in diameter, sometimes over 5 mm. The heaviest rain comes from cumulonimbus clouds. Mountain ranges tend to increase rainfall, which can last continuously for more than 24 hours. Showers usually produce more rain and larger raindrops, but are normally short-lived. Drizzle consists of water droplets less than a millimetre in diameter. It is usually produced by stratus clouds. It often occurs in conjunction with mist and fog, and is always present in hill fog (or scotch mist).

Solid precipitation can come in a variety of forms. Snow is the first of these, sometimes mixing with rain to produce sleet. Other forms include hail (up to 5 cm in diameter), soft hail (2–5 mm) and ice needles.

Dew, hoar frost and rime are also forms of precipitation. They are produced when water vapour is cooled by direct contact with the ground. This results in condensation, either into liquid as dew, or into solid form as hoar frost or rime. When sailing in freezing temperatures, there is always the danger of icing. This happens when water from splashing and spray freezes onto the boat. The colder the air, the stronger the wind and the higher the waves, the heavier the icing. The same effect can be produced by rain which freezes on impact. This is known as freezing rain or glaze.

The **rain-gauge** is an important instrument for the measurement of precipitation. It usually gives rain measurements in fractions of an inch and in millimetres.

When cold air advances across a warmer sea, this encourages the formation of cumulus congestus clouds with their associated shower activity. This is particularly characteristic of the waters between Britain and Iceland, and is especially common in winter months. The fewest showers are produced when the wind is in the south-east. By contrast, winds from west to north-westerly directions produce the most shower activity. Statistical analysis has shown that showers are commoner by day than by night in this important sea area.

Visibility

Visibility is affected by haze, mist, fog, cloud and rain. Visibility can be estimated over lakes and rivers by observing the banks and any

Visibility is adversely affected by all types of mist and fog.

similar landmarks. Over the open sea the horizon is often the only means of estimating visibility, if there are no other ships, lightships or similar objects in sight. In coastal waters the shape of the coast and the presence of such landmarks as lighthouses and church towers can also be helpful.

When estimating visibility you should always take into account the difference in the visibility of different colours. Darker areas will always seem more distant, and light areas closer, than in reality. Lighthouses are often deceptive, causing sailors to overestimate the visibility.

Here is a synopsis of the different visibility levels:

Visibility levels	Distances visible	Designation
0 – 3	**0 – 1,000 m**	**fog**
0	0 – 50 m	thick fog
1	50 – 200 m	moderate fog
2	200 – 500 m	mist
3	500 – 1,000 m	light mist
4 – 5	**1,000 m – 4 km**	**poor visibility**
4	1,000 m – 2 km	haze
5	2 km – 4 km	slight haze
6	**4 km – 10 km**	**moderate visibility**
7 – 9	**> 10 km**	**good visibility**
7	10 km – 20 km	moderately good visibility
8	20 km – 50 km	very good visibility
9	> 50 km	excellent visibility

N.B. 1 metre = 1.1 yards   1 km = 0.6 mile = 0.5 nautical mile

There is also a scale for the measurement of cloud heights:

Cloud level	Actual height in metres
0	0 – 50
1	50 – 100
2	100 – 200
3	200 – 300
4	300 – 600
5	600 – 1,000
6	1,000 – 1,500
7	1,500 – 2,000
8	2,000 – 2,500
9	>2,500 or cloudless

When judging visibility you must take account of cloud conditions, wind, and the temperature difference between the water and the air near the surface. This is particularly important when estimating conditions over sea and coastal waters. On lakes you will notice that visibility is improved in strong winds. In contrast to this, light winds are associated with fog, haze and moderate to poor visibility.

There are a number of useful publications dealing with visibility. Friedrich Nagel gives some important information in his pamphlet entitled *Visibility over West German Waters and the Kattegat*, which applies equally to British waters:

'Winds from SSW are generally associated with the poorest visibility. These winds bring with them warm, moist air, which is cooled as it approaches cooler waters, raising the humidity level and lowering visibility. The best visibility is experienced in winds from NNW. Although these winds are damp and salty, they are warmed as they approach relatively warmer seas, thus lowering humidity and improving visibility. NNW winds are normally associated with the cold, showery airstreams which follow low-pressure areas. Such airstreams are characterised by good visibility.'

The interaction of atmospheric pressure, temperature and wind

This section is extremely important. It is essential to demonstrate to what extent weather is dependent upon the interaction of various meteorological elements. Mere observation of the barometer or of the clouds alone will not give sufficient information on which to base a weather forecast. Other factors are also involved. For example, air movement is determined by two main factors:

1. Temperature differences between cold and warm air masses.
2. The rotation of the earth.

All temperature differences bring about a movement in the air. The principle can be observed at home in the winter. If the back door is opened, cold air flows into the kitchen, while warm air flows outside into the garden. The warm air is lighter. It therefore rises as it flows out through the open door. The cold air, being heavier, flows in across the floor. This circulation produces a draught, the presence of which can be proved experimentally with a match or a candle.

A similar type of circulation is produced globally between the polar and equatorial regions of the earth. Warm air flows out from the tropics towards the poles, while cold air moves from the polar regions towards the equator. This circulation is permanent, thanks to the temperature differences which exist between the poles and the equator.

This circulation also occurs on a smaller scale between areas which warm up and cool down differently:

● between oceans and continents (monsoons);
● between sea and land (sea and land breezes);
● between mountains and valleys (mountain and valley breezes).

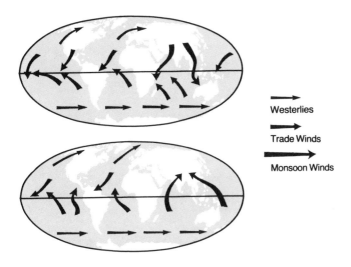

→ Westerlies

➡ Trade Winds

➡ Monsoon Winds

The most important of the world's wind systems in January (above) and in July (below).

If it were not for the rotation of the earth, we could assume the following situation in the Northern Hemisphere: a continuous south-ward stream of cold air on the surface, together with a continuous northward stream of warm air at a height of approximately 5,000 m. However, the situation is considerably modified by the earth's rotation.

The earth rotates on its axis once every 24 hours. This causes all air movements in the Northern Hemisphere to be deflected to the right, and all air movements in the Southern Hemisphere to the left. This phenomenon is known as the Coriolis effect.

Air masses are affected differently, depending on latitude:

- a stationary air mass at the equator moves through 40,000 km every 24 hours as the earth rotates;
- a stationary air mass at the north pole merely turns on its own axis.

This influences the speed and direction of air movements. When an air mass is drawn together horizontally a swirl of air is produced. In the Northern Hemisphere the air will twist in an anticlockwise manner or cyclonically. When an air mass expands horizontally a swirl is also produced, but the air will twist in a clockwise manner or anticyclonically. These swirling masses correspond to low- and high-pressure areas:

cyclonic swirl = low-pressure area (cyclone, depression or low);
anticyclonic swirl = high-pressure area (anticyclone or high).

A **low-pressure area** or **depression** is produced when a part of the earth's surface is warmed more rapidly than the surrounding area. The warmed air becomes lighter and rises. Higher up, the air moves away from the low, sinks again and is drawn back into the low.

The air sinks in the high-pressure area on the right, and rises in the low-pressure area on the left. On the surface the wind blows from the high to the low. Higher up it blows in the opposite direction.

A **high-pressure area** or **anticyclone** occurs when a part of the earth's surface is cooled more rapidly than the surrounding area. The cooled air becomes heavier and sinks. The air flows away from the high along the ground, rises and flows back into the high.

Because of the nature of their origin, these are known as thermal highs and lows. The rotation of the earth and the resulting Coriolis forces produce a clockwise motion in the high and an anticlockwise motion in the low. This results in an exchange of air between lows and highs. Higher up, the air flows from low to high, while on the surface it moves from high to low.

The wind swirls into the low from all sides, and swirls out of the high into the surrounding area.

The wind strength depends upon several factors:

1. The pressure differences between highs and lows.
2. The latitude and the related Coriolis effect. The Coriolis force is nil at the equator and greatest in middle latitudes (40 – 50°).
3. The friction between the air and the earth's surface. The wind is slowed and deflected by friction.
4. The degree of distortion of the path of the wind.

The air is warmed variably, as has already been shown. Air temperature does not decrease uniformly with height. There are parts of the troposphere where temperature actually rises with height. In other words, warmer air masses can rest upon colder ones. These so-called **inversion layers** can extend horizontally, thus blocking the movement of any convection currents from below. This can be observed in the development of cumulus clouds. When a growing cloud reaches an inversion layer it stops rising and begins to spread horizontally. Such inversion layers can occur at any level in the troposphere, and block the vertical circulation of air.

When air masses of different temperatures lie on top of one another we can make certain assumptions about their degree of stability. If heavier cold air rests on a warmer, lighter air mass, the situation will be an unstable one and the weather will be changeable and unsettled. If, however, lighter warm air rests upon a layer of cooler, heavier air, the weather will remain relatively stable. The distinction between stable and unstable air masses is very significant in the study of weather. Any vertical differences in temperature should always be carefully noted.

Turbulence

Sailors prefer the wind to be as steady as possible. But there are often situations in which the prevailing winds are unexpectedly interrupted by gusts and squalls. Such turbulence is particularly characteristic of convection currents and thunderstorms. Gustiness can also be produced by irregularities in the bank, the coastline or the nearby land areas. These are known as **orographic** factors.

Sailing is not affected by small gusts. If they have a diameter of less than 10 metres and last less than 30 seconds, they can be ignored. However, stronger gusts will have an effect on sailing mobility. They can vary between the gusts produced by a bubble of warm air (or thermal) to the squalls associated with a thunderstorm. Here is an outline of the factors involved:

Type of turbulence	Diameter of turbulence horizontal	vertical	Duration of turbulence
Thermal	50 m	250 m	up to 10 minutes
Cumulus convection	500 m	2,000 m	up to 30 minutes
Thunderstorm	20,000 m	10,000 m	up to several hours

The movement of air near the water surface is vital for the propulsion of a sailing vessel. The air up to a height of 20 m is most important for sailing. The wind in this surface layer is influenced by friction, which in turn depends upon the distance from the water surface. As the sea becomes rougher, the wind speed decreases near the surface, but increases higher up. The wind at a height of 15–20 m is often twice as strong as that at the surface. Up to wind force 4 the water surface remains smooth from an aerodynamic point of view. When the water is smooth, any vertical differences in wind speed and direction are of no consequence. If atmospheric conditions are generally stable, there is little turbulence. Unstable atmospheric conditions produce increased turbulence. For example, cold air invading a layer of warm surface air from above will produce very gusty conditions.

Sunny weather and light winds are necessary for the formation of **thermals**. Any obstructions to airflow will also contribute to produce local temperature differences. Such obstructions might include towns or bridges near the shores of lakes. In coastal waters they might be cliffs, bays or islands. The surface air need be warmed by only $1-2C°$ above the temperature of the surrounding air for a thermal to form. Ideal conditions for thermal development are marked alternations between light and shade.

The air rises vertically in a thermal. But there is no cloud formation, which is why thermals are so difficult to observe. A thermal may at the most be betrayed by a wavering of the air, and a gentle onshore gust when the thermal lifts from the ground. When a row of thermals develops along the shoreline, this will quickly produce a freshening onshore breeze. Calm air can be transformed into a force 2 breeze within a matter of seconds.

The formation of a thermal as the ground is warmed. The growth of the thermal depends on the nature of the terrain, and is essentially a local phenomenon.

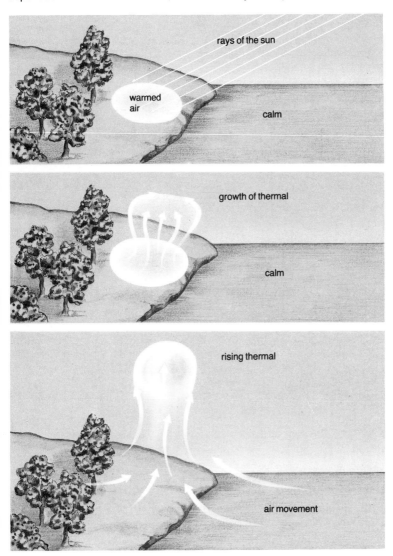

The next step in the development of turbulence is the formation of a **convection cell**. As has already been said, the typical convection cloud is the cumulus cloud. It may also arise from advection, when obstructions such as mountains or cliffs force the air to rise. This always involves the movement of cold air over warm air or a warmed water surface. The turbulence in the surface air will grow in proportion to the size of the convection cell (see the outline on page 61).

Gusts could be described as elements of the wind in the upper air which penetrate to the surface. The following should be noted in this connection:

> The wind in the upper air veers (turns clockwise) relative to the surface wind. So in a gust the wind veers and then backs as the gust recedes.

K.-H. Bock describes turbulence in detail in *Der Wetterlotse*. He makes the following observations about the identification of turbulence: 'It often happens that a pocket of sinking air breaks into the rising air of the convection cell. It thus forms a tongue of turbulent air (a gust). The wind veers and freshens briefly, then backs again. Only about 20–30 seconds later does the turbulence proper set in. This phenomenon is a very useful means of predicting turbulence.'

The time interval between each gust is as important as the strength of the gusts themselves. If T is the interval between gusts, then the following formula applies (according to K.-H. Bock):

$$T \text{ (s)} = \frac{\text{horizontal diameter of convection cell (m)}}{\text{average apparent wind speed (m/s)}}$$

From this formula we can calculate the following, given that we know the average apparent wind speed:

1. The diameter of the convection cell, given the time interval between gusts.
   Diameter of convection cell (m) = T (s) × apparent wind speed (m/s)
2. The interval between gusts, provided we can estimate the size of the convection cell.

Particular attention should be paid to **turbulence in thunderstorm cells**. Violent squalls are associated with the wedge of cold air which marks the outbreak of the thunderstorm. This is preceded by a light breeze, which is directed back towards the approaching storm. Following the squalls the wind backs to follow the path of the storm. The wind drops and then veers as the storm passes. For further information see page 77.

Mention has already been made of the influence of local topography in the section on thermals on page 60. This is particularly noticeable on lakes and rivers, where air movements are partially obstructed by buildings and vegetation on the banks. They create additional friction with the air, producing much increased turbulence.

The type of partial obstruction posed by neighbouring buildings and vegetation is especially dangerous when sailing near the shore. Gaps and corners encourage the formation of eddies. Gusts of 10 knots and more can develop at distances of 50 – 100 m from the obstruction.

Enormous concentration is involved when windsurfing in gusty conditions.

Cliffs and nearby mountains can provide protection from turbulence, but this depends on weather conditions. In stable conditions the shore zone usually remains free of turbulence. When the weather is unstable, however, the opposite is true. Sudden invasions of cold air will combine with local obstructions to produce violent squalls.

Considerable attention must be paid to mountains, cliffs, defiles and similar irregularities. There is a simple rule of thumb:

> Always make enquiries locally about the effect of local geography on the behaviour of the wind.

Airstreams

An airstream is generally uniform in its behaviour. The atmospheric conditions in a particular location will change noticeably only with the arrival of another airstream. A new airstream can take over within a very short time. This is particularly true over the open sea and over flat land, where there are no obstructions to air flow. It is always amazing, for example, to note how quickly an airstream can advance across the North Sea and into the continent, reaching the mountains of Central Europe in a matter of hours.

Airstreams bring with them their own characteristics of temperature and humidity. Atmospheric conditions will change accordingly. Humidity will increase or decrease, atmospheric pressure will rise or fall, temperature will rise or fall. Weather conditions are thus closely bound to the large-scale movement of air masses. It is therefore not enough to forecast the weather on the basis of a rising or falling barometer.

When reading a weather map (see page 112) it is very much a question of identifying the movements of cold and warm air masses, and of correctly estimating their effect on the weather.

Jet streams

The atmospheric conditions in the higher levels of the troposphere are another important matter for consideration. The air pressure and wind conditions in these layers play a vital role in the development of weather patterns.

The lows and highs, which are so important in determining weather, extend up into the higher troposphere. They are, so to speak, propelled from above. The area between 5,000 and 6,000 metres is of particular interest. Atmospheric pressure in these regions remains at around 500 mbar; which means that about half the mass of the earth's atmosphere lies below this level.

At heights of between 5,000 and 6,000 metres conditions are quite different from those near the surface. The air here is only very slightly influenced by conditions at the surface. The global distribution of warm and cold air masses can be observed at this height without interference. The only influence to be felt is the yearly climatic cycle, which is produced by the distribution of oceans and continents.

Wind speeds can be considerable at these heights. Speeds of 150 – 200 kn have been measured at places above 5,000 m. These winds follow well-established paths known as **jet streams**. One jet stream is of particular importance to European weather. It forms a path from west to east through Ireland, Wales and England to north Germany and Poland. Scientists have demonstrated that lows (or depressions) travel enormous distances along the paths of jet streams. It should be noted here that jet streams do not keep strictly to their normal routes. They often form unexpected kinks, which in turn affect the behaviour of the depressions below them. Jet streams also tend to suck up air from the associated depressions. This has the effect of intensifying (deepening) the depressions, which results in heavy rainfall and strong winds.

A tip for the weather buff:

The movement of the jet stream is shown by the movement and behaviour of the highest clouds in the troposphere, namely the cirrus clouds. Their movement will indicate the path of an approaching depression. Stand with your back to the wind: if the cirrus clouds are moving from left to right, crossing the path of the lower clouds, this is a sign of bad weather to come.

Yet more information can be gleaned from the directions of cloud movement. For example, if the cirrus clouds are crossing the lower clouds from right to left (again with one's back to the wind), this means that a depression has just passed. If jet streams and surface winds are blowing in the same direction, this shows that the weather is likely to remain settled.

Typical winds and wind systems

If there is one question about the weather which is of burning interest to all sailors it is this: what winds blow where and when? One or two typical winds have already been described in connection with particular types of weather. Thunderstorms have been mentioned, for example, together with the general problems of turbulence which plague all sailors. I have also tried to make clear the importance of temperature differences and the rotation of the earth in the development of winds. The complex interaction of jet streams and surface winds is responsible for the development of a whole range of typical winds and wind systems. These I shall now explain in more detail.

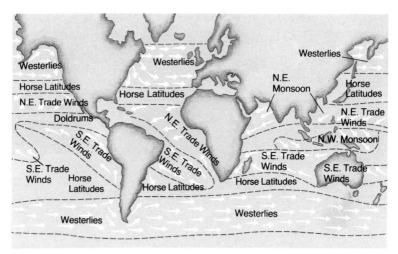

The most important winds and wind systems across the world. The map shows the prevailing pattern for the period from January to March.

The global wind system

There are two important factors here:

1. The amount of heat received from the sun.
2. The rotation of the earth on its axis once every 24 hours.

The intensity of the sun's rays will vary according to season and latitude. The equator will become hottest, the poles coldest. This will tend to produce rising air with low pressure at the equator and sinking air with high pressure at the poles. This holds true for the surface air, but in the upper air the opposite applies. This is because the atmospheric pressure falls less with height in the hotter equatorial regions than in the colder polar regions. The surface air will therefore tend to move from the poles towards the equator, while the upper air flows from the equator towards the poles.

However, the system does not function as simply as that, thanks to the rotation of the earth. The Coriolis force tends to deflect the upper air as it moves out from the equator. By the time it reaches the 30th parallel ($\pm 30°$) the deflection is so strong that the air is moving from west to east. The airflow is blocked, and the air sinks to produce a high-pressure zone at the surface. The earth is thus circled by two high-pressure belts, one in each hemisphere. They are known as the **horse latitudes**.

In this way the earth's rotation has broken the flow of air between the equator and the poles. It is also responsible for a westerly flow of air in the temperate zones between the 40th and 60th parallels. Also, the surface winds which blow from the polar high-pressure zones are deflected to the east. Our own latitudes are characterised by the meeting of warm and cold air masses, resulting in instability with frequent wind and rain.

The equatorial region is very humid, with correspondingly high rainfall and frequent thunderstorms. This zone is known as the **doldrums**, so called because of the sluggish winds and calms which predominate here. The high pressure in the horse latitudes is dynamic in origin. In other words it is produced by air movements and not by differences in temperature. In the summer the continents are warmed to produce thermal lows, which divide these subtropical belts into large areas of high pressure.

Between the horse latitudes and the doldrums run the **trade-wind** zones. The weather is stable here. So too are the winds, which blow with an even strength of 15 kn from the horse latitudes to the doldrums. Their direction is north-easterly in the Northern Hemisphere and south-easterly in the Southern Hemisphere. Stable weather also means that the atmospheric pressure keeps strictly to the daily cycle (see page 14). The slightest irregularities in the daily pressure cycle should be watched carefully, as the majority of tropical storms originate in the border zone between the trades and the doldrums (see page 86).

The doldrums, the horse latitudes and the trade-wind belts move north or south depending on the position of the sun. They move on average through 10 – 15°, reaching their northernmost position in September and their southernmost latitudes in March.

The mechanism of the global wind systems was extremely significant in past centuries, when all seagoing vessels relied on the wind for their propulsion. See also the map on page 68.

Terrestrial winds

In contrast to the global wind system, terrestrial winds are **seasonal** in nature. They owe their origin to the different warming rates of oceans and continents. They are also known as **monsoons**.

Particular weather patterns are associated with monsoon winds:

● In the summer the continent warms rapidly, producing a thermal low. The pressure over the nearby ocean is relatively high. The wind blows from the sea to the land.
● In the winter the continent cools rapidly, producing a high. The pressure over the sea is relatively low. The wind blows from land to sea.

The Indian monsoon is well-known. In the summer it blows from the south-west, across the Arabian Sea and into the Indian sub-continent. In the winter it becomes a dry wind, blowing from the north-east and out over the Arabian Sea. The chart opposite gives a summary of the more important monsoon areas in the world.

Wind conditions are very variable in the period of transition between summer and winter monsoons. There is frequent alternation between calm and turbulent weather.

Monsoon-like winds can also occur in temperate latitudes. They too are related to the different thermal properties of land and water.

This phenomenon is true of many European summers. While the sea warms gradually, the land is heated more rapidly by the sun. An area of low pressure forms over Eastern Europe, with high pressure over Britain and the surrounding sea. A north-westerly airstream is produced, which brings cold, damp weather into Central Europe. If this pattern sets in permanently, a cold, wet summer is the result.

The situation is different in the autumn. The warming of the continent ceases. The sea, on the other hand, continues to store up the warmth gained over the summer months. High pressure forms over Eastern Europe, while low pressure persists over Britain. A south-easterly wind blows off the continent. The situation over Central Europe is one of dry, stable autumn weather.

Land and sea breezes

Monsoons are seasonal winds, affecting a large area. Land and sea breezes are only local daily phenomena, but are very important for sailing.

They are due to the daily warming and cooling of the land. The sea is hardly affected by these changes, and remains much the same by night as by day. The warming of the air in the daytime causes it to rise and the pressure over the land to drop. The air flows in over the land and a sea breeze results. At night the land cools, the air sinks and the

Sea area	Season	Wind direction	Average wind force (Beaufort Scale)
Indian Ocean	Summer	SW	6 – 7 10 max.
	Winter	NE	4
South China Sea	Summer	SE	4 5 – 7 max.
	Winter	NW	4
North Australian coast	Summer (Southern Hemisphere)	NW	4
	Winter	SE	4
Atlantic Ocean: Gulf of Guinea	Summer	W	5
Indian Ocean: South African coast	Summer (Southern Hemisphere)	E	4
	Winter	SW	5 – 6
Pacific Ocean: West coast of Central America	Summer	SW	4
	Winter	NE	4
Atlantic Ocean: North African coast	Winter	SE	4
Eastern Mediterranean	Summer	NW	3 – 4

pressure rises. The surface air flows out over the sea as a land breeze.
Here are a few rules of thumb:

1. The sea breeze sets in at some distance from the shore, and then gradually advances towards the coast.
2. Use the sea breeze when putting into harbour. Daytime is best for this.
3. The land breeze is strongest just before sunrise. It is not usually as strong as the sea breeze.
4. Use the land breeze when putting out to sea. Night is the best time for this.

71

You should use a spinnaker for running before the wind. However, this course should be avoided in high winds or heavy seas.

5. Land and sea breezes are stronger in tropical latitudes. This is because the temperature differences between day and night are greater. The same applies to summer days in temperate latitudes.
6. Sea breezes are also indicated by the pattern of cloud behaviour. Cumulus clouds form in the rising air over the land. They move outwards over the sea, then dissipate as the air sinks again.

Land and sea breezes are not limited to coastal areas. Even lakes can produce sea breezes if the sun is shining strongly enough, and for a long enough period.

Drainage winds

Land and sea breezes owe their origin to the different warming rates of land and sea. Drainage winds, however, are caused by the shape of the landscape, and normally occur in mountainous regions. They are also known as **catabatic** winds.

A drainage wind is produced as the land cools. The resultant cold air is heavy, and tends to sink. It drains into the valleys, which accentuate the effect by funnelling the air. Catabatic winds can be particularly strong where mountains are covered with ice and snow.

Drainage winds can be accentuated by the direction of the prevailing winds. They are particularly characteristic of the regions bordering the Alps, but can be found anywhere where there are mountains. There now follows a more detailed description of some of the most important drainage winds.

Sea breeze

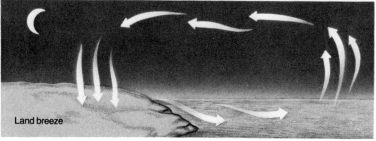

Land breeze

Land and sea breezes are caused by the differing thermal properties of land and water. Unlike the monsoons with their seasonal changes, land and sea breezes go through a daily cycle. In fine weather the land warms rapidly during the morning, producing a low. A breeze blows in off the sea. As the day progresses, the temperature differences begin to even out. By late afternoon or evening the sea breeze has dropped. At night the land cools more rapidly than the sea and forms a high. The air flows out over the sea, producing a land breeze.

The föhn

This wind is most pronounced in the valleys bordering the Alps to the north. It is normally associated with a warm southerly wind, and is characterised by its extreme dryness. This used to be attributed to a warm wind from the Sahara. In fact, the föhn owes its warmth and dryness to another phenomenon, which I shall now attempt to explain.

Warm, moist air is drawn in from the Mediterranean. It is forced to rise by the mountains, and cools rapidly, producing heavy rain, with snow at higher levels. As the water vapour condenses it releases latent heat (this is explained on page 39), which slows down the cooling process. By the time the air reaches the northern slopes of the Alps, most of the moisture has been left behind as rain or snow, and the wind is cold and dry. This wind is increased in strength by the drainage effect, and by the funnelling of the valleys. It also warms rapidly on descent, reaching higher temperatures than before. The warming reduces relative humidity still further to make the wind hot and very dry. Local topography encourages turbulence, sometimes producing record gusts.

The föhn is a particular hazard to sailing in the lakes bordering the Alps to the north. However, föhn winds can occur wherever the right conditions apply. In Britain, such winds are commonest on the north coast of Wales and over the Moray Firth. They are normally associated with a mild, moist south-westerly airstream, which produces a föhn in the lee of mountains. The effect is relatively slight, but has been responsible for record high temperatures in January.

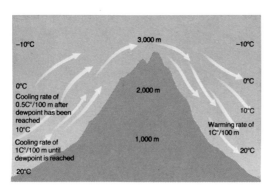

The föhn is produced in the following way. Moist air is drawn in from the south side of the Alps. It is forced upwards, and cools at a rate of 1 C°/100 m until it reaches the dewpoint temperature. From this point onwards the cooling rate is reduced to 0.5 C°/100 m, because of the release of latent heat as the water vapour condenses. Most of the moisture in the air is lost through condensation to cloud, rain and snow, leaving the air dry. As the air descends on the northern side, it warms at a rate of 1 C°/100 m. As a result the descending air becomes warmer than the moist air on the southern side. Humidity is also further reduced as the air is warmed.

The bora

The bora is a drainage wind which originates in the Yugoslavian coastal range (Dinaric Alps). It blows from an easterly or north-easterly direction onto the Adriatic Sea. It is produced by very cold mountain air, and strikes cold in contrast to the relative warmth of the Adriatic. This is because the warming effect of descending air is not sufficient to counteract the chill.

The bora can reach storm force at times on the Yugoslavian and Albanian coasts, but is considerably weaker by the time it reaches the Italian coast. It is an extremely gusty wind, throwing up short, steep waves. These can be very dangerous for sailing.

The temperature difference between mountains and sea is greatest in the winter. At such times the bora can blow on and off for weeks on end. By contrast it lasts in the summer for only a few hours, or a day at the most.

The bora can be further strengthened by a difference in the atmospheric pressure between the mountains and the sea. It is therefore strongest and most persistent when high pressure predominates over the Balkans and low pressure over the Adriatic. Winds of force 9 – 11 are then possible. At such times the cold wind is also usually accompanied by heavy rain.

Some typical drainage winds.

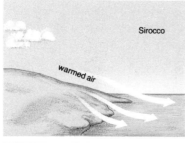

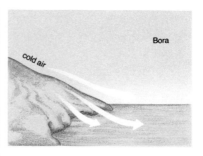

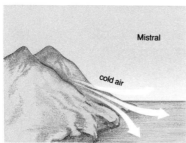

Above left: the sirocco — a hot, dry wind from the south or south-east, mostly occurring in the western Mediterranean.

Above right: the bora — a cold, dry wind from the east or north-east, occurring on the coast of Yugoslavia.

Left: the mistral — a cold, dry wind from the north or north-west, encountered in Provence and along the Italian Riviera.

Heavy cloud formation over the coastal range is a sure sign that the bora is on its way. So when sailing you should always keep a wary eye on clouds over the mountains. You will notice that the clouds move fast in the wind but disperse as they descend to the warmer air below.

The mistral
This wind is similar in origin and behaviour to the bora. It is encountered on the French and Italian coasts between the Rhône and Genoa. A cold north-westerly wind, it blows off the high plateaux of the Maritime Alps. It is also strongest and most persistent in the winter months, when atmospheric pressure and temperature differences are most marked between the mountains and the sea. Winds can occasionally reach storm force, and are usually extremely gusty.

The mistral is also frequent in the spring. It blows once a week on average over the year. In the winter and spring it is normally strongest in the early afternoon; in the summer it is strongest in the morning.

The Rhône valley has the effect of funnelling the air to produce even stronger winds. When the pressure over the western Mediterranean is low enough, the mistral can sweep a long way out to sea. Gales and storms can be experienced as far afield as Sardinia and the Balearic Islands.

Cold drainage winds are by no means confined to the mistral and the bora. They are common wherever there are mountains and deep valleys. The Norwegian fjords and the Scottish lochs are common sites. The notorious helm winds which blow off Cross Fell in Cumbria are perhaps the best example. You should be particularly wary of such winds when sailing on mountain lakes, as they are frequently accompanied by gusts and squalls.

The sirocco
The sirocco (or scirocco) is a hot wind, and similar in type to the föhn. It is usually brought about by low pressure over the western Mediterranean. The depression draws hot air from the desert and over the Atlas Mountains. The mountains tend to make it even hotter and drier. Temperatures of over 40°C (>100°F) are not uncommon.

The sirocco is not associated with any particular season. It can last for hours or even days, and often reaches gale force over the sea. Gusts and squalls are common, and are sometimes accompanied by whirlwinds and waterspouts. A strong sirocco will transport sand and dust from the Sahara.

The name sirocco is also given to another wind which blows in the eastern Mediterranean. Like its western counterpart, this wind is hot and squally, but differs in being damp and muggy. It is strongest when a depression moves from the Mediterranean into the Black Sea. The wind normally blows southerly, veering to westerly.

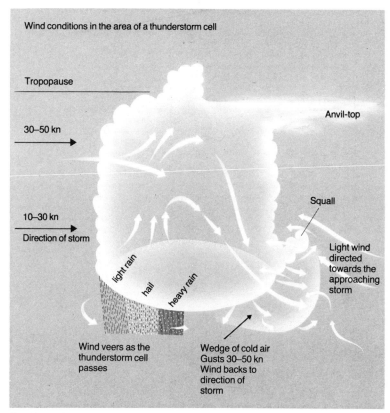

Wind conditions in the area of a thunderstorm cell

Tropopause

Anvil-top

30–50 kn

Squall

10–30 kn

Direction of storm

Light wind directed towards the approaching storm

light rain

hail

heavy rain

Wind veers as the thunderstorm cell passes

Wedge of cold air
Gusts 30–50 kn
Wind backs to direction of storm

A schematic representation of the normal wind conditions associated with the passage of a thunderstorm cell.

Thunderstorms

Thunderstorms are interesting in a number of ways:

● the electrical activity, marked by thunder and lightning;
● heavy rain, accompanied by hail;
● the wind, which is variable and squally, often bringing nasty surprises for sailors.

There are two main types of thunderstorm: the heat (convectional) thunderstorm and the frontal thunderstorm.

Care is called for in conditions like these. Heat thunderstorms usually strike suddenly.

Heat thunderstorms

These storms usually occur on hot summer days. The surface air becomes very hot. It rises sharply, penetrating the cooler air above. Cumulus clouds bubble up, piling into cumulonimbus giants. Strong upward and downward air currents develop in the clouds. Water is continually evaporated and condensed, transporting heat and humidity to higher and higher levels. This process causes the clouds to become electrically charged. The huge thundercloud is visible for considerable distances. It is shaped like an enormous cauliflower, with a fibrous, anvil-shaped top, made of ice crystals.

On the whole, a heat thunderstorm does not bring about a change in the weather pattern. The storm plays itself out, with thunder and lightning, heavy rain and hail. Even snow can occur in mountain regions. The thunderstorm is typically heralded by squalls. The convection currents produce a suction effect, which draws in the air from all directions. Squalls develop from this, which often move backwards towards the approaching storm.

Heat thunderstorms are rarer over the sea than on land. In the tropics they are a regular feature of the rainy season.

Frontal thunderstorms

These storms come about when two contrasting air masses meet. Cold air collides with a warmer air mass, forcing it sharply upwards. The boundary between the two air masses is known as the **front**. K.-H. Bock describes the situation in *Der Wetterlotse*:

'Thunderstorm activity occurs over a much wider area than with heat thunderstorms. It can extend for up to 12 miles either side of the weather front, and for hundreds of miles along the length of the front. The reason for this is that one storm will set off a chain reaction. The cold air in the lee of one storm leads to further instability and the formation of a new storm cell. Thus whole lines of thunderstorms develop, each one creating a new neighbour as it dies out.'

The general accumulation of cloud along the weather front makes it difficult to identify individual storm cells. The approach of heavy rain is often the best indicator.

Wind strength and direction in thunderstorms

The winds associated with thunderstorms are extremely variable (see the diagram on page 77). The event begins in an apparently harmless enough fashion, with the 'lull before the storm', a light breeze directed towards the approaching storm. It freshens quickly, because of a strong updraught created by convection currents within the storm cell.

The heaviest squalls set in immediately the storm breaks. The wind veers sharply as a wedge of cold air thrusts forward. This is known as the **squall line**, and is associated with a sudden downdraught of air. The atmospheric pressure leaps up and the temperature drops sharply. The wind backs noticeably as the squalls pass. They are followed by a massive drop in pressure accompanied by heavy rain. The wind remains gusty as the rain is followed by an area of hail. This usually occurs to the left of the centre of an approaching thunderstorm.

A hailstorm must be avoided at all costs. To avoid hailstones it is essential to know in what direction the storm is moving. The centre of the storm cell should then be kept firmly to larboard. K.-H. Bock gives the following advice on this point:

'If there is a freshening breeze from behind as the storm approaches, then the storm centre is straight ahead. You should determine the movement of the storm cell from the behaviour of the medium-level clouds. This is because the lower clouds will already be affected by convection currents. Whenever thunder threatens you should always keep a careful watch on the movement of medium-level clouds.'

People never fail to underestimate the suddenness with which thunderstorms strike, or the strength of the associated squalls. The 1978 European Soling Championships on the Kieler Förde are an example of this. The second day of this event began with 'ideal sailing weather' and a moderate force 4 breeze. Apparently, dark clouds formed within the space of a few minutes, and a sudden squall ensued. According to the journal *Yacht*, none of the champion yachtsmen present had even foreseen the incident, let alone estimated the strength of the squall. Winds gusted up to force 9 – 10, and four of the solings sank.

Gales and storms

European weather is changeable in nature. Our weather pattern is determined throughout the year by the passage of a long series of lows (depressions). They develop along the so-called **polar front**, the boundary between the warm air of the horse latitudes and the cold air of the polar regions. The depressions alternate with ridges of high pressure. This means that the weather is normally changeable rather than consistently bad. Sometimes one of these ridges will develop into a stable area of high pressure (an anticyclone). The result of this will be a period of fine, settled weather.

The life-story of a depression is of particular interest to sailors, as it is closely bound up with the development of gales and storms. It begins when a tongue of cold air breaks through the polar front into the warmer air mass. This produces a wave formation in the polar front. Atmospheric pressure drops at the crest of the wave, forming a low. Winds circulate round the low, driving the polar front yet further into the warm air. An area of warm, moist air is formed, moving gently eastwards. This is known as the **warm sector**. The part of the polar front lying in front of the warm sector is known by meteorologists as the **warm front**. The part of the front lying behind the warm sector is called the **cold front**. The warm sector is characterised by mild south-westerly winds. The cold front usually moves faster than the warm front. The polar air behind the cold front thrusts forward beneath the warm-sector air, pushing it upwards. In an old depression which has begun to fill, the cold front has caught up with the warm front, producing an **occluded front** or **occlusion**.

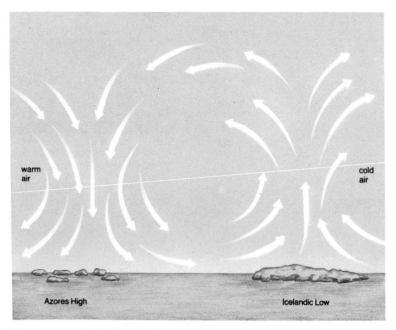

warm
air

cold
air

Azores High

Icelandic Low

European weather is characterised by an alternation of warm and cold air masses. They are derived from the subtropical high-pressure belt (Azores High) and the subpolar low-pressure trough (Icelandic Low) respectively.

The passage of a depression goes through several stages:

1. **Ahead of the warm front**: Cirrus clouds are visible in the western sky. They thicken to form a cirrostratus layer. The pressure falls. An easterly wind veers southerly. Clouds become lower and thicker and it begins to rain.
2. **At the warm front**: The wind veers south-westerly, becoming force 4 – 5. The rain stops and the pressure stabilises.
3. **In the warm sector**: The weather remains cloudy or fair, with haze. A warm wind blows from the south-west. Cloud banks in the west warn of approaching cold air.
4. **At the cold front**: The wind veers north-westerly, becoming strong and gusty. Showers and thunderstorms break out. The temperature falls steeply. The atmospheric pressure drops sharply, then begins to rise.
5. **Behind the cold front**: The wind and rain let up. The weather clears generally.

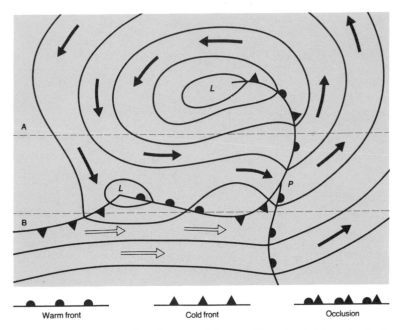

Warm front	Cold front	Occlusion

A depression typical of those which cross Europe. The cold air (shown by black arrows) blows harder, sharply undercutting the warm air (shown by white arrows) and thrusting it upwards. Where the cold front catches up with the warm front (at P), this forms an occlusion.

A = cold sector, B = warm sector, L = low or depression.

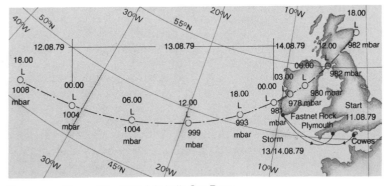

Stormy conditions at the 1979 Admiral's Cup Race.

The wind is strongest immediately behind the cold front. The atmospheric pressure is lowest at the cold front itself. If the temperature difference between the warm and cold air masses is greater, then the pressure is lower and the depression more long-lived. The pressure difference between the centre and edge of the depression is greater, and the winds stronger. In other words, the more intense the depression, the stronger the winds and the more likely a storm or hurricane.

One special feature of some depressions is the **trough**. This is where the centre of the depression lies behind the cold front; in some cases a long way behind. In depressions like these the lowest pressure is encountered half a day or more after the cold front has passed. The wind drops, only to become stronger than ever when the trough arrives. Troughs frequently produce severe storms. Note the following:

> If the wind drops without a rise in atmospheric pressure after the cold front has passed, watch out! The real storm is yet to come.

Troughs can produce some very dangerous storms. One example was the disaster which hit the 1979 Admiral's Cup Race, which cost the lives of 32 yachtsmen. The path of this storm and the route of the race are shown on the map opposite. J. Püttker reported the relevant details in *Der Wetterlotse*:

'The wind strengthened as the trough approached, reaching gale force 8 by midnight. The storm continued, veering westerly, up to the morning of 14 August. The force 11 gusts which swept through the Fastnet region during this period were definitely responsible for the many broken masts. However, the enormous number of broken rudders in the neighbourhood of Fastnet Rock can be attributed to local sea conditions. During the period in question, waves reached a height of 6 m (20 ft) and a period of 8 – 10 seconds in the open sea off Ireland. Individual waves could have easily topped 10 m. Height, however, is not the most dangerous feature of waves, but rather their steepness, and the frequency of breakers.'

The sudden shallowness of the sea in the Fastnet region, coupled with the rocky Irish coast, would have produced a confused sea state with steep waves. Such conditions must have proved extremely destructive to the yachts. Troughs can produce storms and dangerous seas, even in the more sheltered waters of the North Sea, and at times of the year when gales are few (May, June or July).

Depressions follow countless different routes across Europe. Some common routes can, however, be identified. They will, for example, tend to avoid high mountain ranges such as the Alps. This is shown clearly on the map on page 85. It remains an open question whether depressions are affected by changes in the global wind systems.

▲
Rescue action during the severe storm which hit the Admiral's Cup Race in August 1979.

Apart from the masts, rudders were the chief casualties. Yachts were left drifting helplessly.

The main routes followed by depressions across Europe.

Route 1: Depressions move from south-west to north-east, passing to the west of Britain and along the Norwegian coast. Storms occur to the west of Britain.

Route 2: Depressions move from west to east, crossing Scotland and southern Scandinavia. Storms can spread into the North Sea and Baltic regions.

Route 3: Depressions move from west to east, across northern England and Denmark into the Baltic. The North Sea is particularly liable to storms.

Route 4: Depressions move from south-west to north-east, passing along the English Channel, across Denmark and into the Baltic. Storms are more common in summer months.

Route 5: Depressions move from east to west, across southern France and into the Mediterranean. From here they branch off into Eastern Europe or the eastern Mediterranean.

Whirlwinds

These are rare in temperate latitudes. Elsewhere they can be frequent and dangerous, not only to shipping. A whirlwind consists of a twisting spiral of air with a vertical axis. The most important types are considered here.

Dust devils

This phenomenon occurs on overheated ground. The rapidly rising air twists into long spirals, forming into whirling columns of air. Sand and dust is sucked up from the ground. Dust devils are only small phenomena, rarely growing to as much as 100 m in height.

Waterspouts

Unlike dust devils, these develop from above rather than below. They form beneath thunderclouds, spiralling downwards towards the surface. A whirlwind results, which more often than not fails to reach the surface. If such a whirlwind reaches the surface of the sea, a waterspout results. Waterspouts and whirlwinds can attain a diameter of several hundred metres, and produce wind speeds of 60 – 100 kn.

Tornadoes

A tornado is simply a whirlwind of tremendous proportions. Tornadoes are commonest in North America, and occur in weather conditions characterised by enormous contrasts between hot and cold air. They are normally associated with squall lines or severe cold fronts. Wind speeds in tornadoes are impossible to measure, as anemometers rarely survive them.

Tropical storms

Whirlwinds and tornadoes are only small in extent, whereas tropical storms (hurricanes, cyclones or typhoons) can measure up to several hundreds of miles across. They can also extend to heights of 4,000 – 6,000 metres. These storms originate mostly over tropical oceans with moist, unstable weather conditions. They are given different names depending on their place of origin:

- hurricanes in the Caribbean,
- typhoons in the Eastern Pacific and the South China Sea,
- cyclones in the Indian Ocean and the South Pacific.

Those unfamiliar with tropical seas might think that such storms are a regular daily feature of sub-tropical weather. But this is not the case, and no sailor should avoid these waters for that reason alone. If only severe storms are counted, the following annual statistics apply: West

Indies 3, Far East 12, Gulf of Bengal 2, Arabian Sea 1, southern Indian Ocean 8, South Pacific 5, West Coast of America 3.

The journal *Yacht* speaks of the normal weather conditions to be found in the Caribbean: 'North-easterly winds of force 3 – 5, mostly sunny with the light cumulus clouds characteristic of the trade-wind zones'.

Considered from a meteorological point of view, tropical storms consist of small but intense depressions (cyclones). They are characterised by the absence of weather fronts, and by the dense concentration of mostly circular isobars. This is an indication of the enormous pressure gradient between the centre and the fringes of the storm, which is also reflected in the terrific winds produced. So strong are they that the Beaufort Scale is not adequate to measure them. Speeds of 150 – 250 kn are quite possible. The wind is also extremely gusty, which accounts for the enormous destructiveness of tropical storms. Remarkably, the centre (or 'eye') of the storm remains calm. This is due to the general wind pattern involved. Because of the high wind speeds produced, air movement is blocked near the centre by centrifugal force. The eye of the storm measures some 10 – 50 km across. It is elliptical in shape, the longer axis corresponding to the path of the storm. In the Northern Hemisphere the area of the strongest gusts is to be found to the right of the path of the storm, whereas it is to the left in the Southern Hemisphere.

If you want further information about tropical storms, there is much expert literature available on the subject. If you wish to sail in regions liable to such storms. you should naturally obtain all relevant information before setting sail. Moreover, regular listening to the daily weather forecasts is all the more essential.

The pattern and behaviour of severe storms is monitored by weather ships and weather stations all over the world. Of particular interest are the statistics which have been compiled for sea areas south of Iceland and west of Ireland and France. Average maximum wind speeds for the winter months in these waters are given as 70 – 90 kn. However, this is on the basis of statistics for the years 1951 – 1967 only. The equivalent figures for the months of May and June are incorrect if extrapolated from the figures for these years alone.

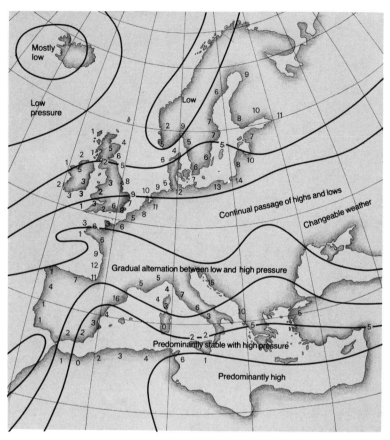

Typical weather to be expected in Europe during the summer. The figures indicate the number of summer days on which thunderstorms are to be expected on the coasts.

Typical weather conditions over Europe

This subject is considered under three main headings:

1. Sea and coastal areas of Western and Northern Europe.
2. Inland lakes of Western and Central Europe.
3. The Mediterranean.

Note that there are publications giving more details about sailing conditions in specific areas. This chapter can only serve to give a

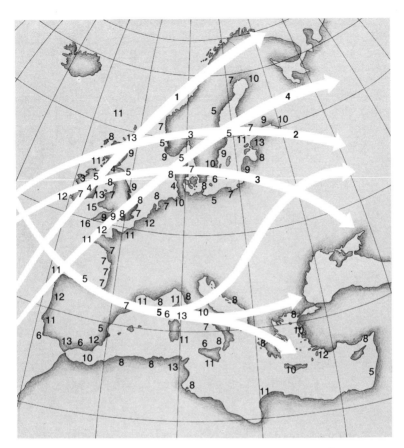

Average annual wind speeds at or near the coasts of Europe and the Mediterranean. Figures are given in knots.

general survey. There will be many exceptions to the general pattern, both in particular places and at particular times.

Sea and coastal areas of Western and Northern Europe

Some typical weather types will be considered here. It should be noted that their influence is not merely limited to the seas and coasts. Rather, the prevailing weather patterns will affect the whole of the neighbouring mainland areas. Even the Mediterranean region will be affected at times.

Westerly conditions

The general situation is determined by a depression near Iceland, and the Azores High, which has a ridge extending across Spain and southern France as far as the Alps.

The weather pattern is extremely changeable over Scandinavia, Western and Central Europe. Showers and longer periods of rain alternate with short clear periods lasting for up to 24 hours. Frontal thunderstorms develop in the summer, and are usually associated with a general deterioration of the weather.

The wind over the sea blows fresh to gale force, predominantly

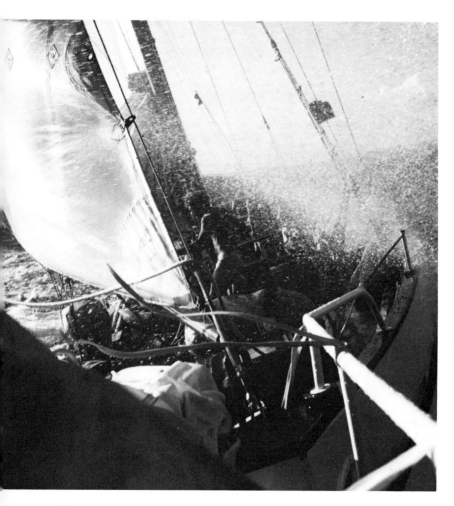

from westerly directions. Average wind speeds amount to 20 – 40 kn. Inland too, the wind remains strong and gusty, especially near thunderstorms. Rainfall and wind strength become less to the south and east.

The weather in the Mediterranean usually remains fine and dry with light winds.

Westerly conditions are commonest in July and August, and least common in March and April.

South-westerly conditions
The general situation is determined by high pressure over southern Russia extending into the Mediterranean, and low pressure over the North Atlantic.

A weather front moves north-east up the English Channel towards Scandinavia and northern Russia. The weather deteriorates generally over Western and Central Europe, becoming persistently wet and unsettled. The rainfall lessens towards the south-east.

The wind over the sea blows fresh to gale force and mostly between south and west. Average wind speeds are 20 – 40 kn. The strong winds penetrate inland, with a strong föhn to the north of the Alps.

The weather in the Mediterranean usually remains fine and dry with moderate winds.

South-westerly conditions are commonest in January and November, and least common in June and July.

North-westerly conditions
The general situation is determined by a high to the west of Biscay and a low to the north of Scotland.

The weather front crosses the North Sea, and moves in towards Eastern Europe. The weather remains wet and unsettled. Showers are frequent and usually squally.

Winds blow between west and north, and may reach severe gale force at times. Average wind speeds are 30 – 50 kn. The bad weather extends inland, with heavy rain over mountains.

The unsettled weather reaches northern Italy, but moves eastwards, barely affecting the Mediterranean.

North-westerly conditions are commonest in July and August, and least common in May and October.

Northerly conditions

The general situation is determined by a high over Britain and a low over Eastern Europe. Unstable cold air brings rain into Central Europe, while Britain and western Europe remain cool but generally dry.

The wind is fresh and gusty over the North Sea and mostly northerly in direction. Average wind speeds are 20 – 30 kn, gusting up to 40 kn in places.

Weather inland remains fine, but with a chilly north wind. In Europe there is heavy rain over the Alps. The cold air penetrates into the western Mediterranean, producing fresh winds, which reach gale force at times.

Northerly conditions are commonest in May and June, and least common in November and December.

Easterly conditions

The general situation is determined by a ridge of high pressure extending from Britain across Northern Europe, and an area of low pressure over south-west Russia and the Mediterranean.

The weather remains fine over much of Western and Northern Europe. In the summer it can become hot, but with minimal thunderstorm activity. The winds remain light, east to north-easterly, which can produce fog off eastern coasts of Britain. Average winds speeds are 10 – 20 kn.

In Central Europe the weather becomes unsettled with cloud and rain, particularly to the east of the Alps. Thunderstorm activity increases to the east and south-east of the region.

The Mediterranean is unsettled too, with wind and rain, especially in the eastern Mediterranean.

Easterly conditions are commonest in April and May, and least common in August and September.

Southerly conditions

The general situation is determined by an area of high pressure over Russia and low pressure over Britain and Western Europe. The weather over Western Europe is generally unsettled with rain. At the same time it is noticeably warmer than usual. The wind is moderate to fresh, mostly southerly. Average wind speeds are 10 – 20 kn.

The weather in Central Europe is less unsettled, but cloudy at times. There is a strong föhn to the north of the Alps, with thunderstorms likely in the summer. The wind can be gusty in a föhn or in a thunderstorm.

The weather in the Mediterranean is changeable and unsettled at times.

Southerly conditions are commonest in December and January, and least common in June and July.

We have just had a general summary of the most important weather types encountered in Western Europe. More details are given below about typical weather conditions to be found over the North Sea. Each map is accompanied by some brief comments. It should be noted that only a general picture has been given. Individual areas and locations will vary considerably in the extent to which wind, waves or fog occur. For example, northern waters are more liable to summer gales than those further south.

Typical weather situations around the North Sea.

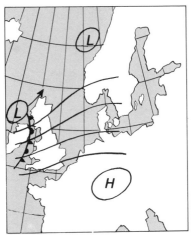 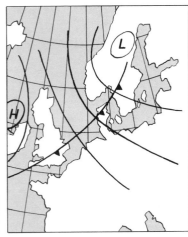

A stationary low off Norway. A low off Scotland moves rapidly north-east. Gales and storms of variable duration.

A stationary high over Ireland and a stationary low over Scandinavia. An unsettled, north-westerly air stream. Gales may persist for days over the North Sea.

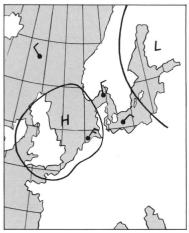

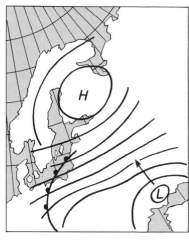

A high over Britain and the North Sea, and a low over Finland. Winds mostly light in the west, but fresh to strong northerly in the east.

High pressure over Finland and low pressure over southern Russia. Easterly gales are possible, even where pressure is relatively high.

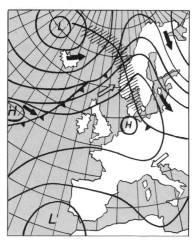

High pressure over northern Scandinavia. A low moves north-west from Eastern Europe. A stiff north-easterly breeze, which backs north-westerly after a day or so.

A typical fair-weather high, bringing settled weather to Britain and Central Europe. Winds variable and light to moderate, though fresher with some cloud over northern Scotland.

An onshore breeze can cause boats to become stranded, even on inland lakes.

Inland lakes of Western and Central Europe

The further inland one travels, the more the weather differs from that over the sea. The continental influence will be felt, even near the coast. The land proves a small but tangible barrier to maritime influences. Local geographical influences will also be more strongly felt inland. Over the continent of Europe, mediterranean influences will be felt to the south, and continental influences to the east.

The Alps form a considerable barrier across Central Europe. They constitute a sizeable orographic obstruction, and will block or deflect the movement of air masses across Europe. Most of the major lakes of Europe are to be found in the neighbourhood of the Alps. They include Lake Constance, Lake Geneva, and the many lakes of Bavaria, Austria, Switzerland and northern Italy.

Many sailors underestimate the weather and wave conditions on these lakes, considering them sheltered and therefore smooth. They forget the variable winds and sudden weather changes which can occur in mountainous regions. Average summer wind speeds of 5 kn (force 2) can mask the frequent squalls produced by föhns, thunderstorms and cold fronts from the north. Wind speeds of 30 – 40 kn (force 7 – 9) are not unknown.

The same applies to the lakes of Britain, many of which lie in mountainous regions (Scottish Highlands, Lake District and North Wales). While föhn influence is negligible, drainage winds are gusty and sudden squalls are common. They can be caused by thunderstorms or by cold fronts. Moreover, the more northerly the location, the greater the likelihood of summer gales.

The influence of local topography on lakes is of considerable meteorological significance. The daily temperature cycles encourage

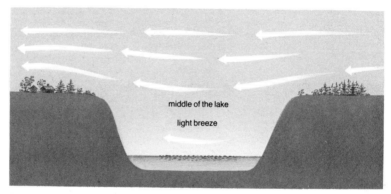

A lake with steep banks: on fine summer days the breeze develops late in the morning, preferring the middle of the lake. Inshore waters remain calm.

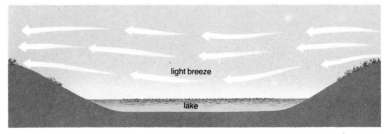

A lake with shallow banks: by early morning the breeze has already reached the shores.

the development of local wind systems. These vary considerably from place to place, depending upon two main factors:

1. The vegetation of the area bordering the shore: woods, meadows and cultivated land all behave differently when they are warmed by the sun.
2. The form and shape of the banks: shallow banks affect the breezes considerably less than steep banks.

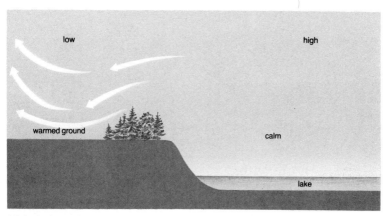

A lake is dependent on its surroundings: a lake surrounded by woods is sheltered from breezes, remaining calm all morning on fine summer days.

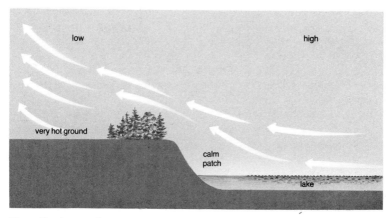

The sailing breeze does not arrive until the afternoon. Even then a calm patch persists inshore.

The development of local wind systems depends very much on these local features. This explains the differences which occur between individual lakes. For example, Lake A may provide better sailing at 8 o'clock in the morning, while on Lake B it may be preferable to wait until 10 o'clock.

The air begins to circulate at sunrise. The local wind systems become reinforced as the day progresses, depending on the height of the banks and the vegetation to be found nearby. You can always tell who knows a lake well. He will avoid calm patches, and sail wherever the breeze is most favourable. If the shore breeze blows in the same direction as the prevailing wind, this is ideal for sailing. If it runs against the prevailing wind, this will slow down the sailing vessel. A few rules of thumb are given here:

1. The breeze always appears first in the centre of the lake.
2. The higher the banks, the longer it will remain calm inshore, and the sooner the breeze will drop in the evening.
3. The onshore breeze is strongest around midday, but varies in strength along the shore.
4. At midday there is light air or calm at the centre of the lake.
5. Take note of how the shores lie in relation to the prevailing wind. Sometimes the onshore breeze will reinforce the prevailing wind; in other places it will counteract it.

These five principles will prove invaluable for sailing on fine summer days. The enthusiast who has thoroughly explored the lake will even find wind when all the other boats are limping along in the calms.

When sailing on lakes, watch out for thunderstorms and sudden squalls, and watch for the föhn in the Alps. Winds can gust up to considerable speeds at times. There are usually plenty of warning signs of approaching storms (see page 54). But occasionally they will strike out of the blue. The most dangerous are the sudden summer squalls associated with cold fronts. This is because their length and intensity are impossible to predict. It is therefore essential to listen to weather forecasts when sailing on lakes, so as to be informed about general weather conditions. If a cold front is forecast it is better to be safe than sorry. Cold fronts can also produce severe thunderstorms, as was explained on page 79.

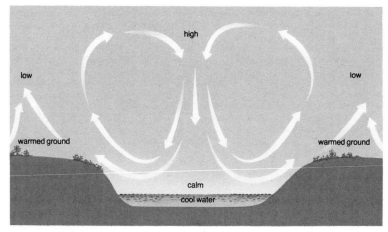

A lake at midday on a fine summer day: the breeze has now moved inshore, leaving a calm area in the centre of the lake.

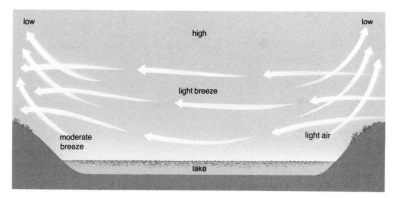

Prevailing winds are strengthened by the onshore breeze on one side of the lake. On the opposite side, however, the onshore breeze weakens the prevailing wind.

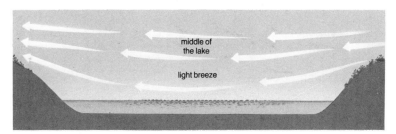

The effect of the prevailing wind varies according to the way the shores lie. However, the middle of the lake always receives more of the prevailing winds.

The Mediterranean

This sea gives its name to one of the world's climates. The mediterranean climate is characterised by hot, dry summers and cool, wet winters. There are a considerable number of mountain ranges near the coasts of the Mediterranean, including the Atlas Mountains, the Apennines and the Dinaric Alps. They accentuate a number of local climatic variations, and produce local winds.

In the winter months the pressure remains low over the Mediterranean, giving generally unsettled weather. In the summer the Azores High pushes out a ridge across the western Mediterranean, while the eastern Mediterranean remains under the influence of an area of low pressure over the Persian Gulf. This situation produces a stable north-westerly airstream across the eastern Mediterranean. These winds are known as the **etesian winds**. There are no marked airstreams in the summer over the western Mediterranean. Winds are thus more variable in these areas.

> **A general rule:** the Mediterranean region is dominated throughout the year by winds from north to north-westerly directions.

Winds are stronger on average in the winter than in the summer. The Gulf of Lions is particularly affected by gales. What is more, they are not entirely limited to winter months, often appearing at other seasons too. Other parts of the Northern Mediterranean are affected by gales in the winter and early spring. They include the Yugoslavian coast (bora), the northern waters of the Aegean, and the southern coast of Turkey.

During the months of July and August, the Mediterranean is mostly free of gales. They can occasionally develop in the Strait of Gibraltar, along the coasts of Algeria and Tunisia, to the south of Sicily and over the Ionian Sea (between Italy and Greece). The Gulf of Genoa and the Aegean Sea are not entirely gale-free either. However, even the stormy Gulf of Lions is relatively calm at this time of year.

Winds will be stronger in areas where the etesians are most developed during the summer. This is especially true of the waters between Crete and Rhodes.

It can be said of the Mediterranean region generally that gales become more frequent in September.

The calmest parts of the region are the waters lying off Egypt and Libya, together with the seas round Cyprus.

Because of the large number of orographic barriers (mountains, islands, bays and gulfs), there is a considerable amount of local wind activity. The map on page 102 gives information on local winds. In this connection, I should also perhaps bring to your attention the chapter on the state of the sea, which begins on page 33.

Western Mediterranean
This area is characterised by east and west winds, encouraged by the direction of the nearby mountain ranges (the Atlas Mountains, the Spanish Sierras and the Pyrenees).

> **Warning:** Prevailing winds can suddenly change direction under the influence of capes and promontories. This will also make the winds extremely gusty.

North African Coast
Here the notorious sirocco blows in from the south. It whips down from the Atlas Range, sometimes carrying sandstorms with it. The sirocco often blows out across the Mediterranean, picking up a

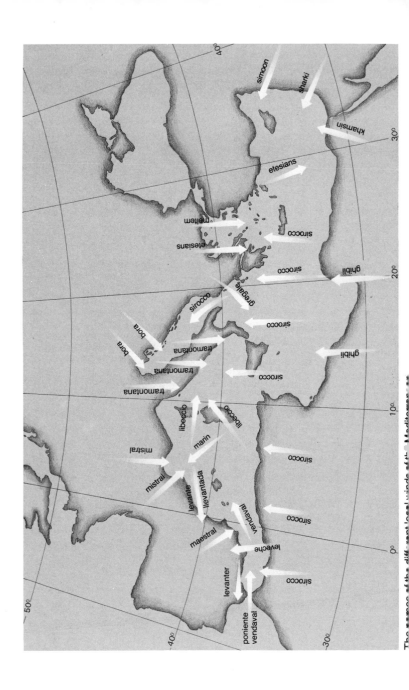

The names of the different local winds of the Mediterranean...

considerable amount of moisture *en route*. The air thus becomes hazy and very muggy.

Northern Mediterranean

Winds in this region are affected by cold northerlies, as has already been explained on pages 75 – 76. The two most important examples of this are the mistral, which often reaches as far as Sardinia and beyond, and the bora in the Adriatic.

Warning: These cold winds create instability, which often releases thunderstorms and squally showers. This phenomenon occurs not so much on the coast itself as some distance out to sea.

Eastern Mediterranean

This region is mostly affected by a north to north-westerly airstream (etesian winds) during the summer months.

The alternation of sea and land breezes is particularly regular on Mediterranean coasts. The sea breeze sets in during the morning, reaching its peak by early afternoon. Evenings are mostly calm. The land breeze usually begins around midnight, lasting until the early morning. The sea breeze is particularly strong when it blows in the same direction as the prevailing wind. The converse can be true, reinforcing the land breeze. It is also quite possible for the sea breeze to be far stronger than the prevailing wind, and from an entirely different direction.

Warning: Individual circumstances produce considerable local differences, which should be known and acted upon.

Visibility

This is generally good throughout the Mediterranean region. Visibility here is 10 km or more on nine days out of ten. The poorest conditions are to be found around the Strait of Gibraltar, where good conditions occur on only eight out of ten days in the summer. Fog is noticeably absent from the Mediterranean. However, visibility can be affected when southerly winds bring sand and dust from the Sahara. Visibility can be reduced at times to between 100 m and 1 km along the coast of North Africa.

When fog does occur, this is usually over the Gulf of Lions or in the Strait of Gibraltar. It occurs when warm, moist air passes over cooler water entering from the Atlantic, resulting in the notorious Gibraltar fogs, with visibility below 50 m. Mirages, on the other hand, can create exceptionally good visibility, particularly along the coast of North Africa.

Cloud and rain

July and August are the least cloudy months in the Mediterranean. The cloudiest areas in the high summer are the Gulf of Genoa and the northern Adriatic. During the same period the waters around Rhodes and Crete are characterised by an almost total absence of cloud. Cloud increases generally in the Mediterranean from September onwards. But even in winter, every third day at least remains sunny.

The frequency of cloud is directly related to rainfall. Winter is the 'rainy season' in the Mediterranean, while summer is predominantly dry. The south-east of the region (Egypt and Israel) suffers total drought in the summer.

When it does rain in the summer, this is mostly in the form of thunderstorms or heavy showers. Both are usually brief but severe. The most thunderstorms occur on Italian coasts. They are also commoner on the east coast of Spain than elsewhere in the Mediterranean. The annual distribution varies generally. Summer thunderstorms are typical of the Gulf of Genoa and the northern Adriatic, while winter thunderstorms are commonest in the south and east of the region. The central and western Mediterranean have the most thunderstorms in the autumn.

While hail can occur in any season over the northern Mediterranean, snow is rare even in the north. There is an average of one or two days at the most. The snow never lingers on the coast. The situation is quite different over the nearby mountain ranges, which can be snow-covered for weeks on end.

The state of the sea

On the whole, wind waves follow the direction of the wind. The wind waves thus move mostly from north-westerly directions. The same is also basically true of the swell. When the wind changes, the wind waves, and eventually the swell, follow suit. The following table gives a rough guide to wave heights in the Mediterranean:

Sea area	Wave heights at gale force 8
Waters around Corsica and Sardinia	3 m (10 ft)
Northern Adriatic	2 m (6.5 ft)
Strait of Gibraltar and Sicilian Channel	3.5 m (11.5 ft)
Waters between Spain and Sardinia	4 m (13 ft)
Aegean Sea	3 m (10 ft)
Waters between Sicily and Greece	4 m (13 ft)
Waters to the west and east of Crete	3.5 m (11.5 ft)
Eastern Mediterranean around Cyprus	3 – 4 m (10 – 13 ft)

Wave heights are on the whole comparable to those in the North Sea. Wind waves of more than 5 m (16.5 ft) are extremely rare in the Mediterranean. On the other hand, a very heavy swell can occur in some sea areas, such as the waters west of Sardinia and off the north coast of Africa. This situation is noticeably more frequent in winter months. The same is also true of any waves between 3 and 5 m.

Warning: In the summer the etesian winds often produce high wind waves and a heavy swell in the eastern Mediterranean, for example between Crete and Rhodes.

Even in the summer, wind waves of between 2 and 3 m (i.e. very rough) must sometimes be reckoned with; to the west of Sardinia, for example, or in the Sicilian Channel, where a 2 – 3 m swell can also occur.

On the whole, the Mediterranean can be considered a relatively 'quiet' sea. On average, eight out of ten summer days will have waves less than ½ m (1½ ft) high.

Warning: There are parts of the Mediterranean, such as the Strait of Gibraltar, where the wind waves run against the sea current. This leads to the formation of short, steep waves. Local geographical irregularities, such as cliffs and shallows, will also influence wave heights.

Temperature and humidity

Winter temperature minima are noticeably higher over the sea than over the land. Air temperatures below freezing are only ever measured near northern coasts of the Mediterranean. Otherwise, temperature minima usually remain between freezing point and 10°C. The hottest part of the year lies between late August and the beginning of September, when temperatures over the Mediterranean rise to more than 30°C. The temperature of the sea itself drops to 5 – 10°C in the winter, and rises in August to 25 – 30°C. On coasts the temperatures differ somewhat from this; inland they contrast even more. The lowest coastal minimum is –15°C at Trieste; the highest maximum is 45°C on the north coast of Africa.

The relative humidity over the Mediterranean lies at around 75% during the winter and between 80% and 85% in the summer. Winds such as the sirocco or the bora can dry out the air, reducing humidity to below 10%.

In the Mediterranean the air can become extremely muggy during the summer, making concentration difficult. What is more, any overnight cooling brings relatively little relief over the sea. August is much the most humid month. The most pleasant climate is to be found in the northern Adriatic at this time. The Aegean Sea too is pleasantly cooled by the etesian winds. The hot, muggy conditions can be particularly unpleasant over the seas around Cyprus. At the height of the summer, humidity can pose problems for sailors all over the Mediterranean region; that is, apart from one or two places on the northern coasts. The table below gives some general indications of the areas which are most favoured climatically at different times of the year.

In July and August, heat and humidity put a considerable strain on the human system. Fortunately the many mountain ranges and other orographic barriers, which so typify the Mediterranean, are beneficial in this regard. They can protect some of the more favoured sailing resorts from the worst effects of humidity. These days it is possible to find accurate information about local humidity levels.

Months	Most favoured regions
January	Coastal areas of Egypt, Israel and Tunisia.
February	As for January, also including Malta, Cyprus and the south coast of Turkey.
March	As for February.
April	Southern Spain, Malta, islands of the Aegean, and coastal areas of North Africa and Israel.
May	As for April.
June	Coastal areas of Yugoslavia, northern Italy and southern France.
July	As for June.
August	As for June, also including the islands and coasts of the Aegean.
September	As for August.
October	Islands of the Aegean, Greece, and coastal areas of North Africa.
November	As for February.
December	As for January.

The weather forecast

Weather forecasts from the media

Radio

The bulk of our weather forecasts are on **Radio 4**. A full weather bulletin is broadcast four times a day. Included in each bulletin is the forecast for the next 24 hours, followed by an outlook for a further 48 hours. A final extra weather bulletin follows the midnight news. This report consists of a summary of the previous day's weather, a detailed forecast for the following 24 hours, and further estimated predictions for the next 5 days. Programmes are also interrupted for gale warnings to shipping. Detailed local forcasts are provided by Radio Scotland, Radio Wales/Cymru and Radio Ulster. Radio 4 VHF also provides a detailed forecast for England in the early morning.

Brief scripted forecasts are broadcast on **Radios 1, 2 and 3**. Radio 3 provides an early morning forecast for inshore waters. Radio 2 programmes are sometimes interrupted to give warnings of severe weather, such as fog, floods, ice or snow.

Local radio stations give detailed local weather forecasts, which vary from station to station.

Television

Regular weather forecasts are provided during the day by the BBC Weatherman, and more detailed local forecasts are provided during regional programmes across the country. A comparable service is provided by the independent TV companies.

The press

All newspapers across the country receive regular weather forecasts from the Meteorological Office. They also receive summaries of the previous day's weather at many coastal resorts. This they publish, together with weather summaries received from major cities and weather stations across the world. Newspapers vary considerably in what information they give and how they present it.

Other services available

Local weather forecasts can be obtained over the telephone. The number to be dialled for this service can be found in the local telephone directory. Weather information is also available via Prestel. Details of this and other services can be obtained from the Meteorological Office in Bracknell, Berkshire.

The international weather symbols are explained on page 117. It is important to read the chapter on the interpretation of weather maps,

which begins on page 112. At this stage, we shall consider in turn each of the elements of the weather which are dealt with in weather forecasts.

Cloud
Information includes the amount of cloud cover present (explained on page 53). The types of cloud and the levels at which they occur can also be shown symbolically. The height of the cloud-base can also be given.

Precipitation
The different types of precipitation are given, together with the amounts which occur.

Temperature
This can be interpreted subjectively by different people, and its significance will vary according to the season. The table on page 109 gives the various terms used for temperatures at different seasons. Some are naturally only used at specific times of the year. The temperatures given here are the daily maxima.

	Maximum temperatures (in degrees Celsius)			
	December, January, February	March, November	April, October	May, June, July, August, September
cold	<0	<2	<4	<8
fairly cold	0 – 2	2 – 6	4 – 6	–
very cool	–	–	–	9 – 13
cool	–	–	6 – 10	13 – 17
normal	~3	6 – 10	10 – 12	–
mild	3 – 8	8 – 12	12 – 16	–
very mild	8 – 12	12 – 16	16 – 20	–
exceptionally mild	>12	–	–	–
moderately warm	–	–	–	17 – 21
warm	–	>16	>20	21 – 25
very warm	–	–	–	25 – 28
hot	–	–	–	>28

Frost is indicated on a five-point scale:

Temperature (in degrees Celsius)	Designation
0 to –2	slight frost
–2 to –5	light frost
–5 to –10	moderate frost
–10 to –15	severe frost
–15 and below	very severe frost

Atmospheric pressure
Figures given include the atmospheric pressure, the change in pressure over the previous 3 hours, and the tendency.

Wind speed
No wind speeds are given in weather forecasts. Wind strengths are indicated by the terms given on the Beaufort Scale, and the effects of the wind are predicted accordingly (see page 18).

Wind direction
It is the normal practice to use only the eight primary wind directions (see page 31). When winds are light they often involve airstreams from several different directions. Changes can also occur within a short space of time. This situation is shown in weather forecasts by the expression **winds light, variable**.

Shipping forecasts

Coastal areas

Special weather bulletins for shipping are broadcast on **Radio 4** at regular intervals during the day. The times of transmission are: 00.15 (approximately), 06.25, 13.55, 17.50. The following items are included:

1. Any gale warnings in force at the time of transmission (see page 116).
2. A summary of the current weather situation as it affects the weather for the next 24 hours.
3. The weather forecasts for the next 24 hours for each **coastal area**. The coastal areas for which forecasts are issued are as follows (in this order):
   Viking, Forties, Cromarty, Forth, Tyne, Dogger, Fisher, German Bight, Humber, Thames, Dover, Wight, Portland, Plymouth, Biscay, Trafalgar (00.15 broadcast only), Finisterre, Sole, Lundy, Fastnet, Irish Sea, Shannon, Rockall, Malin, Hebrides, Bailey, Fair Isle, Faroes, South-east Iceland.
4. The most recent reports received from **weather stations**. The number of stations whose reports are actually broadcast depends on time available. They may include: Tiree, Sumburgh, Bell Rock, Dowsing, Goeree, Varne, Royal Sovereign, Channel Light Vessel, Scilly/Round Island, Valentia, Ronaldsway, Malin Head (also Jersey if time allows).

Area forecasts will include details of wind speed and direction, weather conditions and visibility. Reports from weather stations will include, in addition, atmospheric pressure at sea level and pressure tendency.

In addition to radio bulletins, weather forecasts for coastal areas are available from **coastal radio stations** via **British Telecom International**. An equivalent service is also available from **Irish coastal radio stations**. Forecasts are for the 24 hours following the time they are issued. Details given include wind speed and direction, weather and visibility (in that order). In order to make them clear and brief, the words 'wind', 'force', 'millibar' and 'visibility' are omitted. They are issued on W/T and R/T. R/T broadcasts are given initially at normal speed, but then repeated at dictation speed.

Inshore waters

Weather forecasts for waters up to 12 miles from the coast are broadcast on Radio 4 at the end of normal transmission time. They include:

1. Forecasts of wind, weather and visibility for the next 24 hours.
2. Reports from coastal stations for 22.00 hours. These include wind direction and wind force, present weather, visibility, and atmospheric pressure and tendency at sea level. Coastal stations from which reports are received include: Boulmer, Spurn Point, Manston, Portland Bill, Land's End, Mumbles, Valley, Blackpool, Prestwick, Benbecula, Stornoway, Lerwick, Wick, Aberdeen. Leuchars.

Radio Ulster provides an equivalent service. Radio 3 also provides a forecast for inshore waters (at 06.55 Monday to Friday, at 07.55 at weekends). However, reports from coastal stations are not included in this.

Gale Warnings

These are included as part of the normal weather bulletins, but are also broadcast independently of them. They are issued whenever it is expected that winds will reach an average of at least **gale force 8**, or that gusts will reach at least **43 kn**. They can apply inland as well as at sea.

The Beaufort Scale is used for the average expected wind force. Gusts are termed **severe gale** if they reach **52 kn** and **storm** if they exceed **61 kn**.

The term **imminent** is used for the period up to 6 hours following transmission; **soon** indicates the period from 6 to 12 hours ahead; **later** indicates forecasts for more than 12 hours ahead.

Gale warnings are broadcast immediately by W/T and R/T from British Telecom International and Irish coastal radio stations. They are issued by BBC Radio 4 as soon as the current programme is over. If the gale warning occurs independently of a news programme it is repeated with the next news broadcast.

Here is an example of a gale warning, which will show the essential features included:

'Gale warning, 21 November, 12.40 GMT. Bailey, Rockall, Malin, south-westerly, severe gale force 9, imminent, veering westerly, storm force 10 expected soon.'

Visual signals

Weather stations also make use of visual warning signals consisting of cones and lights. They indicate that a gale is forecast within the next 12 hours or has already struck. The signals apply to the coastal area in which the station is situated. The signal is removed when the wind drops to below gale force, but only provided it is not expected to return to gale force within the next 6 hours.

The signals are used as follows. The **North.Cone** indicates gales expected from a direction north of the east–west line. This is displayed as a cone pointing upwards, or at night by a triangle of lights with the apex pointing up. The **South Cone** signals gales from a direction south of an east–west line. It is represented by a downward-pointing cone, or at night by a triangle of lights with a downward-pointing apex. The cones are changed if the winds are expected to change to the other side of the east–west line.

These visual signals only provide a limited amount of information. If you see them, you should always make further reference to more detailed weather forecasts and gale warnings.

Signals of a visual or acoustic nature are also employed on some inland waters. It is always advisable to obtain accurate information about what local warning systems apply.

The weather map

The weather map is a vital tool for the meteorologist. It is prepared according to a specific procedure. A whole range of symbols is used, which must be understood to make sense of the information presented.

Weather stations across the world provide the important meteorological data from which daily weather maps can be constructed. Whereas in the past it was a difficult and painstaking task to draw up such a map, the process has now become considerably quicker and more sophisticated with the aid of computers.

Firstly, the meteorologist must decide what data are required for the map he intends to construct. These will include detailed measurements of pressure, temperature, humidity and wind. Further information may be added, such as cloud cover and precipitation.

Individual weather stations provide regular reports, giving information under the following headings:

Cloud cover
Cloud types
Cloud heights (including cloud-base)
Atmospheric pressure
Pressure change during the previous 3 hours
Tendency (rising or falling)
Air temperature
Wind direction
Wind strength
Visibility
Dewpoint temperature
Amount of precipitation during the previous 6 hours
Weather in the previous hour
Weather in the previous 6 hours

The weather reports received are entered in symbolic form according to the system laid out below (the symbols are explained on page 117). Measurements and observations are made at specific times by the various weather stations, mostly at hourly intervals. The figures

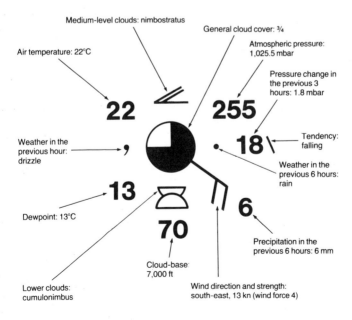

An example of a weather-station report.

obtained are sent by telephone or radio to the Central Meteorological Office in Bracknell (there is an equivalent in most countries).

An internationally-agreed code is used for weather communications. The data are coded in numbers, which are then presented in groups of 5 figures. The coding of all weather reports enables the communication and mapping of weather data to be carried out more speedily. Here is an example from the Meteorological Office, reproduced by permission:

03776 41470 82312 10077 20064 40007 58012 72165 8682/ 333 81812
85656 88458

Numbers in bold type are indicators.

03776	International station number (Gatwick Airport).
41470	No precipitation data; manned station, weather reported; lowest cloud 300 – 600 m AGL; visibility 20 km.
82312	Total cloud amount 8/8; surface wind from 230° 12 kn.
10077	Air temperature 7.7°C.
20064	Dewpoint 6.4°C.
40007	Corrected mean sea level pressure 1,000.7 mbar.
58012	8012 decodes as a fall of pressure of 1.2 mbar over the past 3 hours.
72165	Present weather, 21, rain during the last hour; past weather, 6, rain in previous 1, 3 or 6 hours (depending on time of observation) and also 5, drizzle, during the time interval concerned.
8682/	Total low cloud 6/8 and type cumulus and stratocumulus; type of medium cloud altostratus; type of high cloud not visible.
333	Indicator group
81812	1/8 cumulus base 1,200 ft AGL.
85656	5/8 stratocumulus base 6,000 ft AGL.
88458	8/8 altostratus base 8,000 ft AGL.

A weather map on which all observations have been entered has a decidedly chaotic appearance. It includes a whole variety of signs, figures, arrows and other symbols. The symbols can be interpreted, but even this is a long way from an actual weather forecast.

To produce a forecast, meteorologists must first analyse the data. The aim of this analysis is to produce a synopsis which can be readily understood. The analysis is begun by noting the following:

1. The changing pressure areas, as shown by isobar movement.
2. The movement of warm and cold air masses, as shown by the movement of fronts.

The formal tabulation of data will then be supplemented by scientific explanations of the weather processes and an analysis of the relationship between the different weather elements (temperature, pressure, humidity, wind).

The data from weather stations provide a basis for the creation of **surface maps**. However, an **upper-air chart** must also be produced in order to give a complete picture. Measurements are obtained from the upper air by the use of **radio sondes**. Upper-air observations are made for the 500 mbar level, and show wind and temperature in the same way as surface maps. Pressure, however, is indicated by the heights (in 10s of metres) at which the pressure is 500 mbar (see page 120). For example, if the pressure is 500 mbar at 5,380 m, the figure 538 is given. Analysis of the upper air allows us to forecast changes in pressure and jet-stream patterns, while that of the surface air enables predictions to be made about weather fronts and air masses.

The weather map provides a weather picture for a specific moment in time, while the weather process itself is continuous. Meteorologists therefore try to determine future changes in weather from the analysed data. A new weather map is thus prepared, giving a projection for a specific time in the future. This is accompanied by a scripted weather forecast. The analysis proceeds on the basis of two main lines of research:

1. Forecasting by means of synoptic rules.
2. Forecasting by means of mathematical equations.

Synoptic forecasting involves the simultaneous consideration of all the meteorological elements. Important factors to be considered are:

1. Previous weather patterns and any theoretical deductions which can be made from them.
2. The distribution patterns of atmospheric pressure, temperature, humidity and wind.
3. The movement and behaviour of airstreams and fronts.
4. The position of the jet stream (see page 66).

The task is a difficult one, because the processes are so interdependent. One modifies another in a series of intertwining chain reactions. As the grid of observation points is not consistent, data distribution is uneven, with frequent loopholes. This leads to errors in the analysis of the weather processes. Weather forecasts on the basis of synoptic rules are therefore not very accurate. At best they have only a 4:1 chance of being correct.

The mathematical approach provides a solution to this problem. Because weather develops according to the laws of physics, it is possible to make weather predictions with the help of mathematical formulae and equations. The calculations involved are so compli-

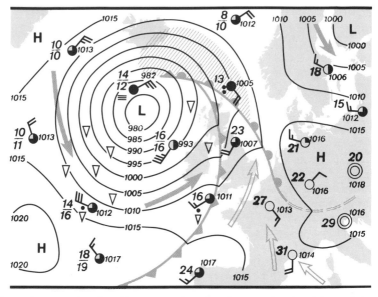

A specimen weather chart. See pages 113 and 116 for an explanation of the symbols. The hatched area indicates rain. Black arrows = cold air. White arrows = warm air.

cated and long-winded that this method has only become feasible with the introduction of computer systems. Meteorologists have been particularly successful in the prediction of jet-stream behaviour. The prediction of wind patterns in the upper air has now become an indispensable component of weather forecasting, and has considerably improved its accuracy.

Radio sondes are essential for the plotting of jet-stream behaviour. They are released into the upper air at regular 12-hourly intervals by 600 weather stations across the world (including eight in Britain). Radio sondes transmit readings of wind speed and direction, atmospheric pressure, temperature and humidity from the upper air. The following important measurements are taken:

1. Height at which temperature is at freezing point.
2. Height at which cumulus clouds begin to form (condensation level).
3. Surface temperature necessary for the formation of cumulus clouds (release temperature).
4. Upper and lower cloud boundaries.
5. Heights of inversion layers.
6. Wind speed and direction at specific heights.
7. Boundary between troposphere and stratosphere (tropopause).

Weather symbols

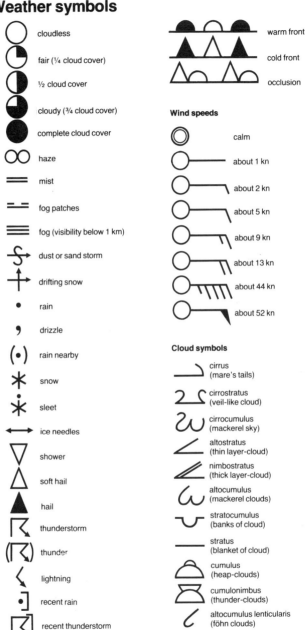

cloudless

fair (¼ cloud cover)

½ cloud cover

cloudy (¾ cloud cover)

complete cloud cover

haze

mist

fog patches

fog (visibility below 1 km)

dust or sand storm

drifting snow

rain

drizzle

rain nearby

snow

sleet

ice needles

shower

soft hail

hail

thunderstorm

thunder

lightning

recent rain

recent thunderstorm

warm front

cold front

occlusion

Wind speeds

calm

about 1 kn

about 2 kn

about 5 kn

about 9 kn

about 13 kn

about 44 kn

about 52 kn

Cloud symbols

cirrus
(mare's tails)

cirrostratus
(veil-like cloud)

cirrocumulus
(mackerel sky)

altostratus
(thin layer-cloud)

nimbostratus
(thick layer-cloud)

altocumulus
(mackerel clouds)

stratocumulus
(banks of cloud)

stratus
(blanket of cloud)

cumulus
(heap-clouds)

cumulonimbus
(thunder-clouds)

altocumulus lenticularis
(föhn clouds)

Weather report for 23 December 1976 at 07.00 hours

Station	Height m	Weather	Wind in km/h	Temperature °C yesterday		at 2 m	dew-point	at night		Sunshine yesterday in hours	Precipitation prev. 24 hrs mm	Snow depth cm
				maximum	average			at 2 m	ground			
Berlin	50	cloudy	calm	4	1.6	–1	–1	–3	–5	0.5	–	remnants
Schleswig	43	cloudy	NNW 7	3	2.2	1	1	1	1	–	–	1
Hamburg	16	fog	WSW 5	5	2.8	1	1	0	–3	2.7	–	1
Bremen	3	fog	calm	6	3.0	–2	–2	–3	–4	2.3	–	
Hannover	55	sunny	ENE 2	6	2.6	–4	–4	–5	–7	0.7	–	
Essen	134	sunny	ESE 7	4	1.7	–2	–2	–2	–5	2.8		

Station	Weather	Wind in km/h	Temperature °C	
			07.00 hours	yesterday maximum
Athens	cloudy	N 29	10	12
Bucharest	cloudy	NNE 7	1	1
Copenhagen	cloudy	ENE 14	2	4
London	cloudy	ESE 9	6	10
Madrid	fog	calm	2	10
Moscow	snow	WSW 4	–4	0
Paris	cloudy	ESE 4	6	7
Rome	cloudy	NE 9	12	15
Stockholm	cloudy	NW 9	–4	0
Warsaw	cloudy	WSW 4	1	2
Vienna	cloudy	SE 16	–0	2
Zurich	fog	NE 4	–3	–3

The data here provide some of the information recorded on the maps on pages 119 and 120.

A section from a weather map produced by the German Weather Service for 07.00 hours (= 0.6.00 hours GMT) on 23 December 1976.

This weather chart is the product of all the weather data available to the German Weather Service for that specific time. The sources of data were the weather bulletins received from stations all over Europe. These bulletins were radioed to central office in the internationally-recognised code. The measurements were then incorporated into the chart by skilled technicians. The process was carried out by means of computers equipped with plotters.

The weather symbols are explained on page 121. Weather maps are sometimes coloured as follows: red line = warm front; blue line = cold front; violet line = occlusion; black lines = isobars; broken line = trough; light green hatching (or dotted area) = rain; dark green hatching (or starred area) = snow; yellow hatching (or shaded area) = fog.

This chart shows the weather at one specific point in time. Meteorologists can use it to determine the current weather situation at 07.00 hours on 23 December 1976, which is described as follows:

'Germany remains under the influence of a weak ridge, running between the Central Russian High and a weak high centred over Denmark. The northern plains are affected by cold air, while the central and southern hill-regions are affected by warm air. In the outlook period the cold front associated with the depression off the North Cape will move southwards, and will affect our weather from Boxing Day onwards.'

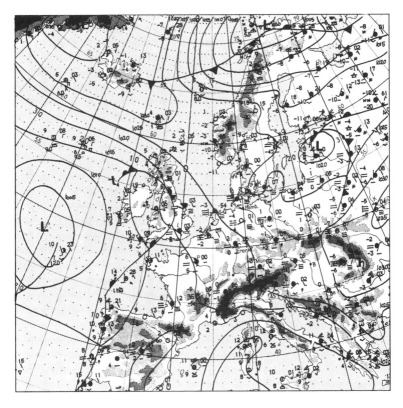

119

A map of the upper air at the 500 mbar level (corresponding to a height of approximately 5,000 m) at 07.00 hours on 23 December 1976, produced by the German Weather Service.

The chart on page 123 represented measurements made at ground level, and gives information about the behaviour of air masses and fronts. This map provides important information about the upper air, and in particular about jet streams and pressure patterns. The upper-air chart is constructed from data received from radio sondes.

Pressure in the upper air is shown by means of isohypses. These are topographical contour lines. Here they mark the heights (in 10s of metres) at which the atmospheric pressure is 500 mbar. They are usually smoother than isobars on the ground, owing to the absence of barriers such as mountains. Upper air and surface air interact in the development of weather.

The upper-air chart should not be seen as a mere continuation of the surface map, for it is formed quite differently. Changes in the upper air filter only gradually to the ground, as is shown by the behaviour of surface depressions. A ridge in the upper air is often found above a powerful warm-sector low on the ground. A high in the upper air usually lies north-west of a low on the ground. The jet stream is shown by cirrus clouds above the warm front.

Lows in the upper air are associated with invasions of cold air. Low temperatures in the upper air produce extremely unstable conditions in the warmer air below, especially in the summer, giving heavy rain and showers.

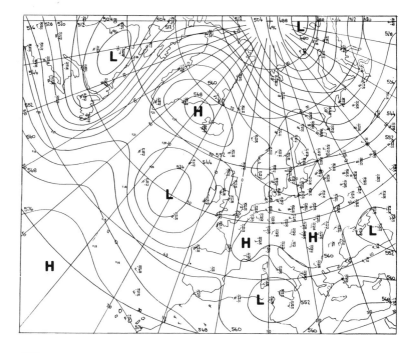

A surface weather map, showing the forecast for 01.00 hours (= 00.00 hours GMT) on 23 December 1976, produced by the German Weather Service.

Page 122 shows some of the weather reports which provide the observational data for the map on page 123. This is further supplemented by the upper-air chart on page 124, which is based on data received from radio sondes. The meteorologist's next task is to provide a weather forecast on the basis of these records. Forecast charts are constructed for this purpose.

The map below shows the forecast for 01.00 hours (Central European Time) on 23 December 1976. It is based, naturally enough, on the analysis of observational data received at 07.00 hours CET on 22 December 1976.

The forecast chart incorporates the expected pressure distribution, together with the anticipated movement of weather fronts and temperature changes. The weather forecast is based on these predictions. You should compare the data shown on this map with the actual observations recorded on the map on page 123.

Newly-formed depressions move relatively quickly from west to east, often covering more than 5,000 miles in 24 hours. They begin to slow down considerably as the cold front closes in on the warm front, eventually producing an occlusion.

The forecast map is accompanied by a scripted forecast for all the individual regions within the forecast area. This concludes with further prospects for the outlook period.

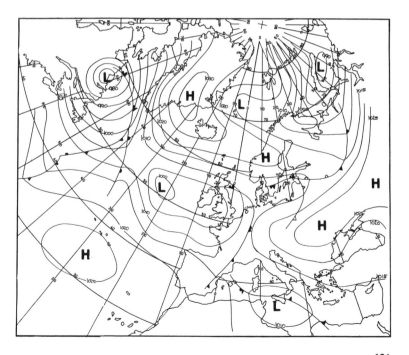

Weather observations on board

When observing the weather on board there are three main sources of information:

- the thermometer (see page 37),
- the barometer (see page 11),
- personal observations of wind and weather.

With practice it is possible to pick up a variety of clues about the weather to expect. Two points should be noted in this regard:

1. Considerable previous experience of this is essential.
2. Observations are always to a certain extent dependent on local circumstances.

Before embarking on unfamiliar waters, it is always advisable first to make enquiries locally about special weather signs to look out for.

The following elements of weather can be aptly and accurately ascertained from personal observations:

Atmospheric pressure	(page 11)
Wind	(page 16)
Clouds	(page 53)
Visibility	(page 56)
Colour of the sky	(page 134)
Swell	(page 35)

Add to that all the sailing experience you have gained in temperate latitudes, and you may begin to make predictions about the weather, such as are laid out on page 133. But no forecast can be certain until every aspect of the weather has been fully and accurately understood. When sailing on the sea you are well advised not merely to rely on weather and shipping forecasts on the radio, but to plot the information on your own weather chart. Most people can better understand the processes involved when they can see them laid out in front of them in visual form.

It is also useful to have a cassette recorder on board. With this you can record all weather reports and play them back for mapping purposes.

A moderate to fresh breeze, force 4 – 5.

Preparation and analysis of weather charts on board

I shall illustrate this with an example, using a specimen forecast. The forecast is a German one, but the same principles apply generally. Our example uses weather observations made on 11 September 1980, which are tabulated on page 125.

The weather forecast for a particular area is based on the maximum possible number of observations, all made simultaneously. Weather observations are made, according to international agreement, at 00.00, 06.00, 12.00 and 18.00 hours GMT. Note that the observations for this example were made at 08.00 hours, Central European Summer Time (CEST) being 2 hours ahead of GMT.

Weather situation:	Reports from weather stations on the .11.09.80, at .11.00...	Forecast today until 24.00 / 12.00 / 06.00	Outlook tomorrow until 12.00 / 00.00 / 06.00

DLF Bulletin on the ..11.:09.:1980...11.09.80...12.40. 01.05. 06.10 Central European Time

Weather situation:
- today 07.00 08.00
- yesterday 19.00
- today 04.00

Depression 998, northern Kattegat, moving east, filling. Cold front 1005 Saxony, 1015 Constance, moving east. Trough 1005 Scheluwer, moving east. Ridge 1020 Scillies, 1015 Central England, moving east, weakening. Large depression 991 56N, 21W, moving ENE, still intensifying. Former hurricane 'Earl' 400 n.m. west of Ireland, moving north-east.

Reports from weather stations on the 11.09.80, at 11.00...
1. Skinna W4 11° 1002
2. Svinoy NNW3 11° 1006
3. Lista NW3 13° 1002
4. Aberdeen NNE1 12° 1011
5. Tynemouth NNE2 13° 1012
6. Hemsby WNW4 14° 1014
7. Den Helder NW5 16° 1010
8. LS Borkum Riff NW8 14° 1006
9. Helgoland NNW5 15° 1001
10. List/Sylt NNW7 15° 998
11. Thyboron N7 13° 999
12. Skagen N7 12° 994
13. Fornaes W3 14° 992
14. Kullen SSW min 13° 993
15. Kegnaes NW5 14° 996
16. Kiel Lighthouse WNW6 14° 996
17. LS Fehmarn Belt WSW6 15° 995
18. LS Møn
19. Arkona WSW5 14° 997
20. Bornholm SW6 shower 14° 996
21. Visby SE5 min 12° 1000
22. Mariehamn SSE1 14° 1004
23. Hel S5 min 11° 1002
24. Ocean Weather E5 min 12° 993 Ship L

Forecast today until 24.00 / 12.00 / 06.00

German Bight: NW to W 7-8, backing, temporarily weakening 6, later SW to S strengthening 6-7, good visibility.

South-west North Sea: Westerly 5-6, backing, strengthening 7-8, good, later moderate visibility, rain.

Central North Sea – West: W to SW 5-6, backing sharply, strengthening 7, moderate visibility, later rain.

Central North Sea – East: N to NW about 7, backing, squally showers, good visibility.

Skagerrak: NE to N about 6, rain, moderate visibility.

Kattegat: W to NW strengthening 7, squally showers, good visibility.

West Baltic: NW strengthening 7-8, later backing, weakening 6, squally showers, good visibility.

Central Baltic: S to SW 6-7, veering, strengthening 7-8, squally showers.

Outlook tomorrow until 12.00 / 00.00 / 06.00

- SE to S strengthening 8-9, veering SW.
- S to SW 9.
- SE strengthening 9.
- SW5, backing SE, strengthening 8.
- NE winds 5-6, later SE, strengthening 7-8.
- NW about 6, backing, temporarily weakening 5, later S to SE strengthening 7.
- SW about 6, backing, strengthening 7-8.
- NW7, backing, weakening 6.

125

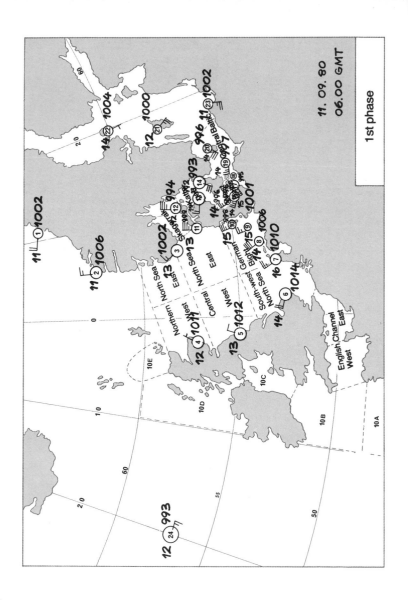

1st phase

Enter the **weather observation data**. Details of wind, weather, temperature and atmospheric pressure are provided by weather stations. For the purpose of drawing isobars later, it is helpful to use as many reports as possible. The map above shows what the chart should look like after the first phase is complete.

126

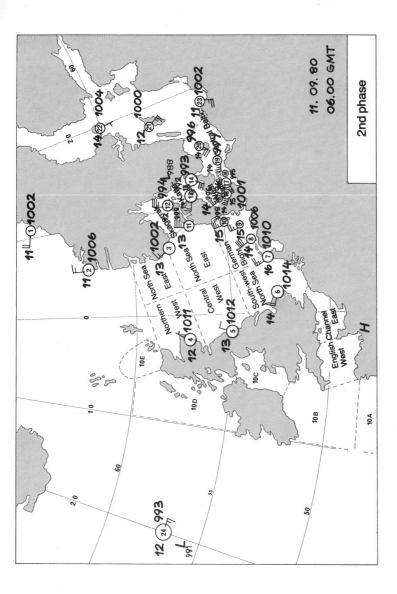

2nd phase

Enter the **positions of pressure foci (centres)** (H = high, L = low). The atmospheric pressure should be entered next to the H or L, for example L_{991}. The exact positioning of pressure foci will assist later in the construction of isobars. If the position of weather fronts is also known, this should also be drawn in at the same time. The map above shows how the map should look following phase 2.

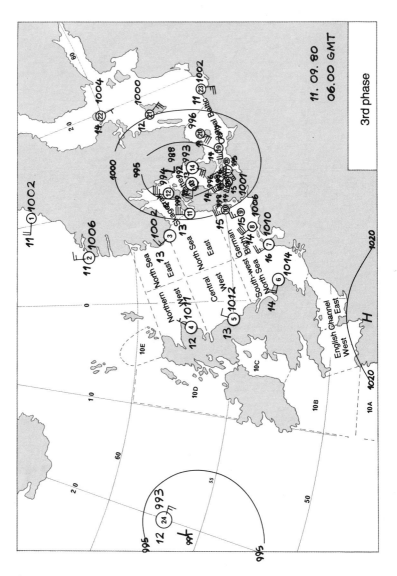

3rd phase

Begin to draw in the **isobars** (see page 15). The pressure readings and wind arrows for the weather stations will help you in this process. You should begin with isobars around well-defined areas of low or high pressure. Isobars should eventually be drawn at 5 mbar intervals. Initially, however, it may be simpler to begin with 10 mbar intervals. After phase 3 is complete the chart should look something like the map above.

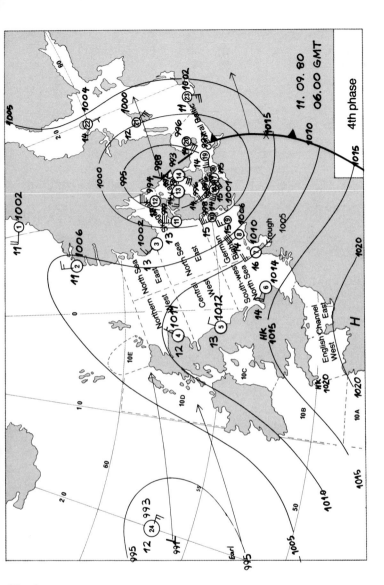

4th phase

Continue to fill in the isobars. Wind arrows should normally run roughly parallel to the isobars. Local wind systems can admittedly produce exceptions to this rule. You should, however, ignore these irregularities and concentrate on the overall pressure distribution. Isobars should be drawn in smooth curves, without any angles. Admittedly, this is not always easy to achieve. The pressure readings from weather stations are the only reference points available. If an isobar passes in between two stations, draw the line through the mid-point. The map on page 129 shows how the chart should look after the completion of the fourth and final phase. Do not forget to enter the date and the time when the observations were made.

How do we continue from here? The map in front of us gives only vague information about the weather for today and tomorrow. More accurate predictions can be made with the assistance of the current weather report in the shipping bulletin (see page 110), and personal observations on board.

Let us assume that the boat is in Kiel. The forecast for the western Baltic at 12.40 hours (for the following 12 hours) runs as follows:

'Squally showers, wind force 6, later strengthening force 7 to gale force 8, from south-westerly directions. In the afternoon, cloudy with relatively good visibility and a slight rise in pressure.'

The log entry on board corroborates this: wind westerly force 6; pressure 1005 mbar; temperature 13°C.

A weak ridge has developed between the retreating depression over southern Sweden and the depression to the west of Ireland. It is already shown on the weather chart, and lies roughly along the east coast of Britain. The extensive depression west of Ireland demands extra attention as it is moving east-north-east and intensifying (deepening). Today's forecast already speaks of winds strengthening force 7 to force 8. Any sailing is quite out of the question, as the wind will become even stronger by tomorrow.

Here is the weather situation as reported on next morning's bulletin:

'A deep depression (980 mbar) over the Hebrides, still intensifying, moving slowly east. A depression (1,000 mbar) in the area of Gotland, moving east-north-east, filling (weakening).'

The map opposite shows the current weather situation at 08.00 hours (CEST). The movement of the depression can be clearly seen. It can be made still clearer by drawing arrows from the pressure foci, showing the direction in which they are moving (see the map on page 129).

By the morning of 12 September the general deterioration in the weather can be observed from on board: gale force 8 backing south-westerly, increasing severe gale force 9. Visibiity is considerably poorer than the previous day. It is now misty.

The regular preparation of personal weather charts on the basis of shipping bulletins makes it possible to follow the movement and behaviour of highs and lows while still at sea. A chart should be drawn up for every weather bulletin. By examining a series of consecutive maps, it is possible to estimate the direction and speed of moving depressions. This can considerably improve the accuracy of weather forecasts.

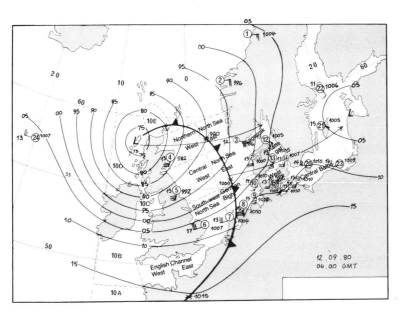

The map on page 85 shows the typical routes of depressions across Europe. This can provide a model with which to compare the actual observed route of the depression in question.

The observation of atmospheric pressure and wind changes from on board can provide a means of checking the forecasts given in weather bulletins:

1. In temperate latitudes, if the wind **veers**, then the depression is passing to the **north** of the boat.
2. In temperate latitudes, if the wind **backs**, then the depression is passing to the **south** of the boat.

Depressions move across the sea at an average speed of 10 – 20 kn. However, rapidly-moving depressions can reach speeds of 40 – 60 kn. If a depression is said to be 'rapidly intensifying', then this also means it will move more rapidly.

Here are a few important general points to be considered when analysing weather charts:

- The warm and cold fronts are the boundaries where warm and cold air masses meet.
- The direction of isobars indicates wind direction.
- The distance between isobars indicates wind speed.
- A depression moves to where the pressure drops most sharply.
- A high-pressure area moves to where the pressure rises most sharply.
- If there is a marked contrast between cold and warm air, the depression is rapidly deepening.
- If the isobars are bunched together where the front crosses them, then the front is moving rapidly.
- If the pressure falls more sharply in front of a depression than it rises behind it, then the depression is deepening.
- If the pressure rises more sharply behind a depression than it falls in front of it, then the depression is filling.

Meteorological navigation

This term is used when a boat accommodates its course to the prevailing weather conditions. Sailing vessels can seldom avoid this. But even steamers follow the rules of meteorological navigation, if only to avoid storm hazards or to economise on fuel.

Meteorological navigation is of primary importance for sea and coastal sailing. Yachting practice incorporates some of its essential features:

- Taking advantage of certain seasonal and daily wind systems.
- By-passing of islands and promontories, while exploiting general climatic and local weather conditions.
- By-passing of gales and hurricanes, and manoeuvring correctly when negotiating gales, storms and tropical hurricanes.

Wherever you sail, be sure to keep a constant eye out for the weather, paying particular attention to:

- atmospheric pressure (page 11),
- wind (page 16),
- cloud (page 46),
- visibility (page 56).

Personal observations on board are no substitute for repeated attention to official weather forecasts. Forecasts made on the basis of personal observation require both practice and familiarity with local weather behaviour. The following rules apply to the conditions generally to be found around Europe.

1. Forecasts based on changes in atmospheric pressure

- A slow and even rise in pressure indicates the approach of an anticyclone (high).
- A slow and even fall in pressure indicates the approach of a depression (low).
- A rapid or very rapid rise in pressure after changeable weather indicates the presence of a ridge. No lasting improvement to the weather can be expected.
- A sharp or very sharp fall in pressure in the summer is a warning of a thunderstorm. Even without a thunderstorm, this heralds a rapid deterioration in the weather, with squalls and gales.

2. Forecasts based on wind speed and direction

- A freshening breeze during the morning, followed by calm in the late afternoon, is characteristic of fine, settled weather.
- Calm or very little wind in the morning, followed by a freshening wind in the late afternoon, is a sign of rain and strong winds to follow.
- If the wind blows from the same direction for days, and then suddenly changes, a change in the weather is to be expected.
- In the summer, the regular cycle of land and sea breezes is an indication of fine weather. Any disturbance in the cycle points to a change in the weather.

3. Forecasts based on cloud formations

- Fine summer weather is characterised by small, loosely-formed cumulus clouds, which quickly disperse.
- Layer upon layer of cloud, if anything stratus at higher levels with cumulus lower down, points to changeable weather associated with a general deterioration in the weather pattern.
- The appearance of a mackerel sky does not necessarily mean a deterioration in the weather.
- The appearance of cirrus cloud, followed by lower cloud, indicates the approach of a depression.

A final word of warning: none of the suggestions given above are any more than rules of thumb. All will have considerable exceptions depending on the locality and the combination of different meteorological factors involved.

Appendix

Questions about meteorology

Now that you have finished this book, you may wish to test your knowledge of the weather. See if you can answer these questions. When you have finished, compare your answers with those provided immediately following the questions. The answers we have given may not be the only possible ones, so check them up by looking at the pages referred to at the end of each answer.

Questions

1
What does this symbol mean on a weather map?

2
What information is provided by the Beaufort Scale?

3
In what units do we normally measure atmospheric pressure?

4
What can you expect if there is a sudden change in atmospheric pressure?

5

What does a sudden fall in pressure signify?

6

What should the weather be like if the pressure falls by more than 1 mbar in the space of an hour?

7

What are the lines which are drawn in circles around centres of high and low pressure?

8

Explain what you see on this chart.

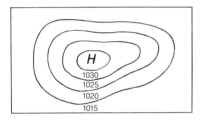

9

Describe what is shown on this chart.

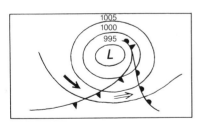

10

From what sources can weather information be obtained?

11

What does this sign mean? ▲

12

What does this sign mean? ▼

13

You hear the following gale warning on the radio:
'South-westerly storm, veering.'
What does this mean?

14

You receive this gale warning over the radio:
'South-easterly gale, backing.'
What does this mean?

15

What is the apparent wind?

16

What information is given in a shipping bulletin?

17

How is the pressure gradient shown on a weather map?

18

Why is a barograph preferable to a barometer?

19

A depression moves from south-west to north-east, passing to the north of your area. How does the wind behave?

20

According to the weather forecast for your area, winds will back during the day. What may be happening to cause this?

21
How does the wind behave around a high and a low in the Northern Hemisphere?

22
How can you work out the whereabouts of a nearby depression?

23
What causes a sea breeze to develop during the day?

24
Describe the formation of a land breeze.

25
Why is the wind always stronger in corners and narrow places?

26
What do you understand by the term **front***?*

27
How is a warm front formed?

28
How does the wind behave when a cold front passes?

29
What kind of weather can be expected in a trough?

Answers

1
A north-westerly breeze, force 3, with no cloud. Low pressure is somewhere to the north of the symbol.
(See pages 19, 31 and 32.)

2
All the wind forces, numbered from 0 to 12, giving details of their effects on the land or the sea.
(See pages 18–19.)

3
In millibars (mbar). Sometimes also in millimetres of mercury (mm Hg).
(See page 12.)

4
A sudden change in weather.
(See page 133.)

5
Bad weather to come, with the possibility of gales.
(See page 133.)

6
There will be gales and storms, possibly with heavy rain.

7
They are called isobars: lines which connect points with the same atmospheric pressure.
(See pages 15–16.)

8
This is a strong anticyclone (high-pressure area). The pressure is given in mbar for each isobar. Isobars are at 5 mbar intervals. They are close together, which indicates a steep pressure gradient and strong winds.
(See pages 15–16.)

9

A depression with a warm front and a cold front. The atmospheric pressure is given for each isobar, and the warm and cold airstreams are shown by a white and a black arrow respectively.
(See pages 80–82.)

10

Weather forecasts on radio and television, in the press and over the telephone; the Meteorological Office; shipping bulletins and weather station reports via radio and British Telecom International.
(See pages 107, 110–111.)

11

This is the North Cone. It warns of gales from a point north of the east–west line.
(See page 112.)

12.

This is the South Cone, which warns of gales and storms from a point south of the east–west line.
(See page 112.)

13.

The wind will be storm force 10, and its direction will be changing in clockwise motion from south-west to west.
(See pages 17–21.)

14

This means that the wind is gale force 8, and its direction is changing anticlockwise from south-east to east.
(See pages 17–21.)

15

The wind which is felt on a moving boat. It is produced by the combination of the real wind and the movement of the boat.
(See pages 20–21.)

16

A statement of any gale warnings currently in force, followed by a general synopsis of the weather situation. Then forecasts for coastal areas (giving details of wind, weather and visibility), and for coastal stations (giving details of wind, weather, visibility, pressure and tendency).
(See page 110.)

17

By the isobars: the closer together they are, the steeper the pressure gradient.
(See page 16.)

18

The barograph not only gives the current atmospheric pressure, it also shows the tendency and any changes in pressure.
(See page 14.)

19

The wind veers (changes in a clockwise direction). For example, it may veer from south to south-west, and then to west.
(See page 131.)

20

There is a depression passing to the south of your area.
(See page 131.)

21

The wind spirals clockwise out of the high and anticlockwise into the low.
(See pages 15 and 60.)

22

Stand with your back to the wind. The low will be slightly ahead of you to the left.

23

The land is warmed, and the air above it rises. The air flows in from the sea to replace it, creating a sea breeze.
(See pages 70–73.)

24

The land cools more quickly than the sea at night. The air sinks, forming a high. The air then flows out to sea.
(See pages 70–73.)

25

The wind is funnelled and deflected, producing an effect like a jet.

26

This is the forward boundary of an air mass. The warm front lies to the front of a warm air mass, while a cold front lies ahead of a cold air mass.
(See pages 80–82.)

27

Warm air encounters a cold air mass ahead of it, and gradually glides above it.
(See pages 80–82.)

28

The wind veers sharply and strengthens, giving gusts and squalls from the west or northwest.
(See pages 80–82.)

29

The pressure falls sharply some way behind the cold front. The wind, which previously veered, backs and strengthens suddenly, often producing severe weather.
(See page 83.)

Acknowledgements

Page nos.

30/31   M. Rodewald in *Der Wetterlotse* nos. 381/382, Sep./Oct. 1978.

44/45   H. Schmidt in *Der Wetterlotse* nos. 381/382, Sep./Oct. 1978.

56/57   F. Nagel: *Visibility in West German waters and the Kattegat* (Monograph No. 66, German Weather Service), Hamburg, 1969.

63/64.   K.-H. Bock in *Der Wetterlotse* nos. 379/380, July/Aug.
77/78   1978.

78   *Yacht*, 30 August 1978.

80/81   J. Püttker in *Der Wetterlotse* nos. 393/394, Sep./Oct. 1979.

84   Krauss/Meldau: *Sea and weather lore for sailors*. 6th enlarged edition by W. Stein and R. Höhn. Berlin/Heidelberg/New York, 1973.
Yacht, 1980, no. 2.

85   *Der Wetterlotse* nos. 383/384, Nov./Dec. 1978.

98   *Mediterranean Handbook* Part III, 6th edition by the German Hydrographical Institute, Hamburg, 1977.

106/107   *Weather advice to the community* (Meteorological Office Leaflet No. 1), Bracknell, 1982.

108   W. Horst in *Der Wetterlotse* nos. 387/388, Mar./Apr. 1979.

110/117   *Weather bulletins, gale warnings and services for the shipping and fishing industries* (Meteorological Office Leaflet No. 3), Bracknell, 1982.

119   *An introduction to the work of the Meteorological Office*, Bracknell, 1982.

123–125   Charts produced by the German Weather Service, Offenbach, 1976.

128–133   German Weather Service: *Ground weather chart no. 9 (1:10 million)*, Hamburg, 1980.

Further information

Reed's Nautical Almanac, London.
Alan Watts: *Wind Pilot: a Yachtsman's Analysis of the Thermal Winds of Europe and the Mediterranean (with Supplements 1–4)*, London, 1975.
World Radio–TV Handbook, London.

Picture credits
Associated Press   p.82
Foto Berger   p.76
R. Denk   p.54
German Press Agency   p.70
Dr F. Krügler   p.21–30,41,44,47,47–51,55
P. Stückl   p.8,34,36,62,88,100,106,109,126,cover
Fa. A. Thies & Co. KG   p.13,14

We thank the German Weather Service (Marine Office), Hamburg, for their kind permission to print various maps of theirs. We also thank the Meteorological Office, Bracknell, for their kind permission to reproduce the table on page 119.